# Letters From India: The Chronicles of a Canadian Family Living in India from 1970 to 1972

**Edited by Jeff Tranter**

First Printing: January, 2023
ISBN: 978-0-9921382-1-9

Dedication:

This book is dedicated to all of the Canadian families that lived in the RAPP Township in Rajasthan, India, supported each other and helped build a close-knit community.

(this page intentionally left blank)

# Table of Contents

(this page intentionally left blank)

# Preface

This book tells the story of a Canadian family (my family) that lived in India for two years from 1970 to 1972. Rather than write the story, it is presented in the form of the letters that were sent to our relatives back in Canada during this period, as well as photographs, postcards, newspaper clippings and other material from the time.

(this page intentionally left blank)

# Acknowledgements

This book would not have been possible without the letters written by my parents for the benefit of our relatives back in Canada. As should be obvious when reading them, an incredible time and effort went into writing, making copies and mailing them out on a regular basis.

My thanks also go to my relatives who diligently kept the letters we sent to them and which were returned, after all this time, along with the original photographs and additional material such as postcards and newspaper clippings.

Jeff Tranter
Ottawa, Ontario, Canada
January, 2023.

(this page intentionally left blank)

# The Format of This Book

The bulk of this book is a series of letters written by my mother and father to our relatives back in Canada. Through these letters you will gain insight into our experiences during that time.

To give some context to the letters presented in the book, I present some background on the reason we were there: the Rajasthan Atomic Power Project, and then a little information about our family.

The book proper then begins, starting with some letters that were sent when on our way to India.

The largest section of the book is a series of newsletters that reported on our experiences during the two years we were in India. This section also includes a sampling of some of the personal letters that were sent at that time.

The Postscript chapter summarizes our trip home, gives some history of later developments in the power project and what the family members are doing today.

The original letters were written by hand or more often typed on a manual typewriter with either carbon copies or spirit duplicator ("ditto") machine copies onto thin air mail paper. After 50 years these have become somewhat faded, so I have transcribed them, keeping most of the original appearance and formatting intact and transcribing the hand-written letters. I have made some minor spelling and grammatical corrections, but for the most part left the letters as they were originally written. I've also included some scanned pages of the original letters for comparison.

Since the letters were intended for our relatives who knew very little about India, I think you will find them for the most part self-explanatory. I have added some footnotes where I thought it was useful to add additional facts, updates, trivia, or other items of interest.

I have also redacted certain personal information and the names and addresses of people outside my immediate family, for the sake of privacy. For example, a name like John Smith will be written as J-- S--.

I really enjoyed this little project. I had never actually seen these letters before and they brought back many fond memories. I learned some things I didn't know, as well as finding that, after more than 50 years, a few things contradicted what I thought I remembered.

(this page intentionally left blank)

# Introduction

## The Rajasthan Atomic Power Project

In the 1950s, Canada developed the CANDU (**CAN**ada **D**euterium **U**ranium) design for pressurized heavy-water nuclear reactors to generate electrical power. The design had some inherent features that made it safer than some other reactor designs and made use of Uranium ore mined in Canada for fuel. Several reactors were built and the Canadian government and industry saw the potential to sell the technology to developing countries such as India that had a growing need for electrical power. By making the initial cost of the reactors affordable (even subsidizing it), the idea was that Canada would profit from selling the fuel and heavy water needed to operate the reactors on an ongoing basis. India agreed to such a program to develop CANDU reactors starting in the 1960s.

The Rajasthan Atomic Power Project (R.A.P.P. or RAPP) was initiated to build a group of reactors in the central Indian state of Rajasthan. The site was well-suited for a number of reasons, including a large body of water needed for the reactor cooling, available electrical power, a nearby town and a location central to where additional electrical power was needed in India.

Building a nuclear reactor is an expensive, complicated and time-consuming undertaking, even in Canada. To do the same in India would require sending Canadian engineers and managers to India, finding suitable local labour and materials to construct it and shipping key components from Canada and sourcing or building others locally.

To support the hundred or so Canadians and their families working on this multi-year project, an entire town was constructed with houses suitable for Canadians to live in and with facilities like a swimming pool, tennis courts, park and a school for students from kindergarten to grade eight.

The 1960s was a turbulent time of rapid social change in woman's and minority rights, a growing interest in nature and the environment and an embracing of different cultures and religions. The culture, fashion, food and music of India was of particular interest to people in the West. Just one example was the trip to India by The Beatles in 1968 to study Transcendental Meditation under the Maharishi Mahesh Yogi. Their music, particularly that of Beatle George Harrison, was influenced by classical Indian music and introduced it to the West. These cultural changes meant that the prospect of a young Canadian family living in India for a couple of years was a much more exciting and appealing opportunity than it might have been a few years earlier and it was not hard to find volunteers.

By 1970, most of RAPP township had been built, the first group of Canadian engineers and their families were living on-site and construction of the first reactor was well underway. Many of the staff came from two small communities where CANDU reactors had already been built and were operating: Deep River, Ontario (near Ottawa) and Port Elgin, Ontario (on Lake Huron). Most worked for either Atomic Energy of Canada Limited (AECL) or Ontario Hydro.

(this page intentionally left blank)

# The Tranter Family

My parents, William ("Bill") and Margaret ("Marg") were born in Toronto, Canada in 1940, the children of immigrants from England and Scotland. Both of my parents became schoolteachers, met and married in 1960. Three children arrived: Jeffrey ("Jeff", born in 1961), Linda (born in 1962) and David (born in 1964). In 1965 we moved from an apartment in Toronto to a new house in the growing suburban community of Malton (now part of the City of Mississauga).

In late 1969 or early 1970 my father, by then the vice principal of an elementary school in Toronto, heard about the opportunity to be the head teacher of a Canadian school in the RAPP township in India. We discussed the idea as a family and my father applied for the position, but we were asked not to tell anyone about it until we heard whether it might actually become a reality.

After some months of waiting we received the news that we were indeed going to be living in India for a two year term and started receiving information about where we would live and what to expect. We also started a long series of immunizations against the various tropical diseases we might be exposed to. We grew quite excited as the time of our move approached.

(this page intentionally left blank)

# The Letters

## On the Way There

We left Toronto for India on July 6, 1970[1], but took the opportunity over the span of a few weeks to visit a number of places in Europe on the way, staying at hotels and spending a few days in each city seeing the sights.

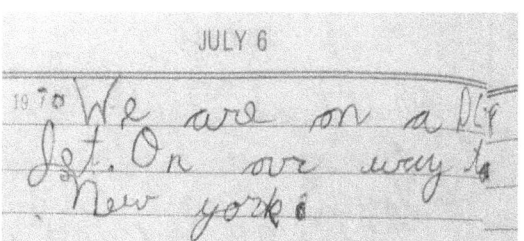

*Figure 1: A page from my diary on the day we left. The diary was a gift from my grandmother before leaving, although I was not very diligent in making regular entries.*

Places visited on the way included a stopover to change flights in New York, then London, England, Paris, France, Rome, Italy, Athens, Greece before arriving in Mumbai, India.

In this section I present some letters sent during the trip there as well as some postcards and photographs.

---

1    On July 5, 1970 an Air Canada flight crashed while attempting to land at Toronto Pearson International Airport. All 100 passengers and 9 crew on board were killed. At the time it was Canada's second-deadliest aviation accident. We left on an Air Canada flight from Pearson the next day. Needless to say, there were no copies of the newspaper provided to the passengers on our flight that day!

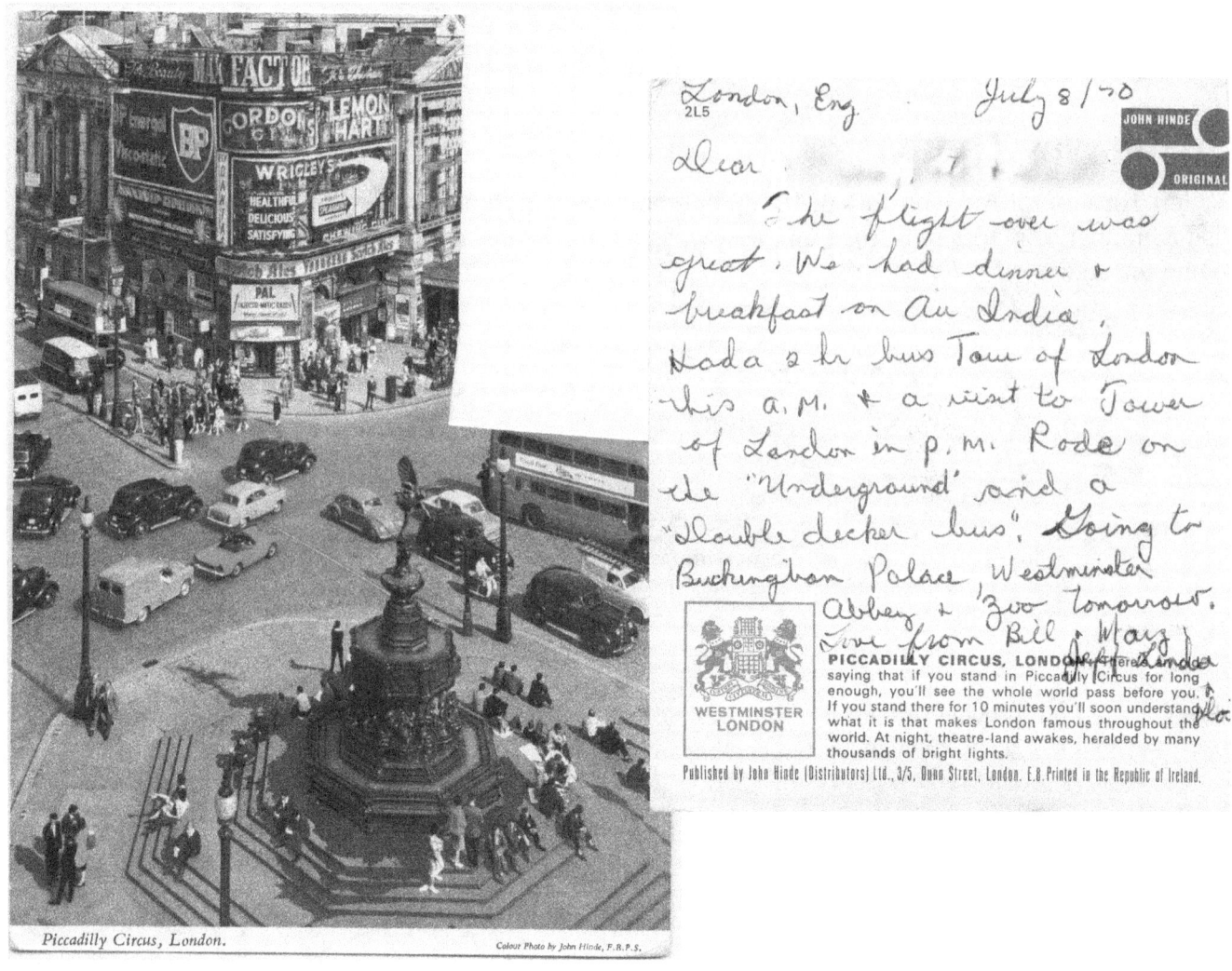

Piccadilly Circus, London.

Colour Photo by John Hinde, F.R.P.S.

*[Transcription of postcard sent from London]*

London, Eng.                         July 8/70

Dear G--, P-- & S--
    The flight was great. We had dinner & breakfast on Air India. Had a 2 hour bus tour of London this a.m. and a visit to Tower of London in p.m. Rode on the "Underground" and a "Double decker bus". Going to Buckingham Palace, Westminster Abbey & Zoo tomorrow.

Love from Bill, Marg, Jeff, Linda & David.

*[Transcription of postcard sent from Paris[2]]*

12me Juillet, 1970

Chères G-- et P--,

Nous sommes à Paris! Notre hôtel est magnifigue mais très chèr. Nous sommes près de l'Opéra et beaucoup des spectacles interéssante. Notre Français est utile mais très faible! Demain nous prenons un tour de Paris au matin et nous visiterons La Tour Eiffel, etc. dans l'après-midi.

      Mardi est le Jour de Bastille, une grand fête francaise! Nous sommes tous en bin état!

Au revoir,
Marg et Guillaume et les enfants!

---

2    The letter was written by Marg to her sister and husband in her best high school French, just for fun.

July 18/70
Athens, Greece

Dear G--, P--, S-- (+ ? yet?[3])

Arrived in Athens this afternoon. The airport is right on the Mediterranean coast. We had a lovely view of the ocean with its many islands, most were like small mountains sticking out of the water. This evening we went for a walk and ended up at the Acropolis high on a hill overlooking the city. We sat at outdoor tables and drank lemonade as the sun set behind the hills surrounding others. I bought a mohair crocheted stole for 20 drachma (approximately 75¢).

Our hotel is very nice, the staff seem to speak enough English to get along and we have an amazing view of the Acropolis from our window. It towers high above the city on a hill (small mountain?) and is lighted at night. Tomorrow morning we are taking a bus tour to see all the historic sights and in the evening going to a "sound and light" show and Greek dancing. We've said several times that P-- would probably appreciate Rome and Athens more than we do because there is so much history that we really don't know about.

Rome was great especially the food. We had pizza, spaghetti, ravioli and a couple of really delicious veal dinners. Food was much cheaper here than in Paris. We took two bus tours in Rome and they were really good. It's the only way to see a lot in a few days. We've seen so many unusual and interesting things that it's impossible to tell anyone about them. We've just roamed down many little back streets, we walked for what seems like miles every day. That's the way to see what a place is really like. You should really save your money and see some part of Europe. It really gives you a different feeling about other countries and how Europeans must feel when they come to Canada where they don't speak the language and understand our customs.

---

3    At the time we left there was a baby on the way.

If we ever do this again I think I'll take a crash course in the languages we'll need. It was really odd tonight to walk down a street packed with people and not understand what they are saying or be able to read the signs. All the street signs are in Greek script and also most of the store window signs.

We're having a wonderful trip, everything has gone as planned except for a 4 hour delay in leaving Paris, but Alitalia served us a nice lunch, so we really couldn't complain. Our air flights have been great with beautiful scenery on arriving in Rome and Athens. Our hotels have varied from luxurious in Paris to adequate in Rome (average for Rome we think). We'll be in Bombay[4] on Tuesday morning and we are really looking forward to that. Will write from there.

Love Bill & Marg, Jeff, Linda, & David.

---

4   Now known as Mumbai.

(this page intentionally left blank)

# Newsletters and Personal Letters

Here follows the largest section of the book – the regular newsletters. Five copies of each were sent out to family and relatives on a regular basis. Letters addressed to individual family members are personal letters (usually handwritten) of which I have included a sampling. The letters are presented in chronological order, interspersed with some pictures, postcards, newspaper clippings, etc.

## IN CASE YOU WERE WONDERING...

### LOCATION:
We will be living in a community about 30 miles from the Indian city of Kota. It is approximately 350 miles south of Delhi in the State of Rajasthan in India. To get some idea of the location, draw a straight line from Bombay on the west coast of India and Delhi in the North, Central India. Kota is located approximately 2/3's of the way up the line from Bombay.

### JOB:
Bill will be teaching in an elementary school with Grades 1 - 8. The school has two teachers and approximately 50-60 pupils. He is head teacher in the school and will probably be responsible for teaching 25-30 pupils at the Grade 5 to 8 level. Teaching responsibilities begin the first week of August, 1970 and end in May, 1972. Pupils are children of Canadian workers.

### HOME:
We will be provided with a 3 or 4-bedroom home with basic furnishings, a stove, refrigerator and two air conditioners. The home is a two-storey brick building surrounded by a wall.

### COMMUNITY:
The community is called RAPP Township (Rajasthan Atomic Power Project). It is located approximately 10 miles from the site of the project on the Chambal river. Community services include a shopping centre, swimming pool, recreation hall, tennis courts, post office, etc. Both Indians and Canadians live in housing built specifically for workers on the RAPP project. The school is located near the centre of the community.

### TRAVEL:
On the way to the site we will visit: London, Paris, Rome and Athens. We leave on July 6th and arrive in Bombay, India on July 21st. After several days in Bombay, we will travel by train (20 hrs.) up to the RAPP Township. Although we have made no definite travel plans for other holidays we hope to see Northern India, Kashmir and major cities within driving distance. We will likely come home via the Pacific in the summer of 1972.

### MAIL:
Postal service by surface mail is slow in India. Parcel post (surface mail) would take up to 3 months to arrive from Canada. Air mail service is approximately 10 days. Mail will be appreciated and answered with either personal letters or news letters. Our address is:

> Mr. W. H. Tranter
> H6/9[5]
> RAPP Township,
> Via Kota,
> Rajasthan, India.

### IN CASE OF EMERGENCY:
In the event of an emergency, contact Atomic Energy of Canada, Ltd., in the Sheridan Research Centre in Mississauga. They will cable the Power Project Site and we will have the message in less than 24 hours.

---

5    The actual house we were assigned was H7/5, as later newsletters mention.

H7/5
RAPP Township
Via Kota,
Rajasthan, India,
August 8, 1970

Dear J-- & L-- & D--,

Well we're finally getting settled in our new home. We hope you will be able to share news with Mom or G-- and P-- occasionally. To overcome the need for sharing, we've sent out the present newsletter with carbon copies for all immediate family. We hope it will get you up to date a bit.

*[some personal details redacted]*

How is everyone in the family? Write soon with lots of news.

Love,
Bill, Marg & the kids.

Prepared by: W.H. Tranter (under the careful supervision of Margaret J. Tranter)

## Why A Newsletter?

We have already discovered that the first person we write to gets the most information. After that, we get tired of writing the same material over and over again. So, this letter has 4 carbon copies. We hope you get a readable one!

## Monsoon Season

Monsoon season (or rainy season) at site has been very unusual this year. Usually there is a great deal of rain falling almost every day. This year, we have had some rain showers and only one heavy rainfall yesterday (Aug. 7th). Some nearby areas will suffer greatly in crop yields unless a fair bit of rain falls in the next three weeks or so. This will have a bad effect on food prices for the people in this area.

Today has been a very hot, sticky day with almost 100% humidity. Clothing washed yesterday is still damp and clothing sticks to you all the time. The temperature is not too high (in the 80's[6]) but most people in the community say this is one of the most uncomfortable times of the year.

## The School

The RAPP Township Canadian School has been operating for a week now. There are 33 pupils with more arriving this weekend. The other teacher (Mrs. W--) has 15 pupils in Grades 1-4 (including David and Linda). Bill has 18 pupils in Grades 5-8 (including Jeffrey). The school has two fair-sized classrooms, 5 smaller study or storage rooms and a fair-sized library. There is a fair amount of equipment. The pupils are excellent workers - much better than most city-school pupils. It is a pleasure to teach them and a real challenge to keep track of four grades all at once!

The school, like most buildings in the community leaks during heavy rains. Yesterday afternoon, there were five puddles on the floor during the late afternoon from leaks in the roof - mostly seepage through cracks in the mortar.

## Boring Evenings?

This week we hoped to have our shipments and air freight consignments from Bombay but they haven't arrived. Both are in Bombay and through customs. We are assured that they are on a truck on the way up to site from Bombay, but they still haven't arrived. As a result we are living on borrowed kitchen utensils and bed linen. We have only the clothes we took with us for Europe and the children

---

6    All temperatures are given in Fahrenheit, as Canada had not yet moved to the metric system at the time.

have only the toys they carried in their kit bag on the airplane. The evenings we have spent at home have been used for reading, talking, school work, etc. All the great games, hobbies, musical instruments, etc. have yet to come. We hope it will be soon!

An air freight shipment of school supplies has been held up at customs because some of the atlases showed the boundaries of the Indian territories differently than the Indian government policy suggests they should. We suggested that they stamp the pages as inaccurate or simply rip the offending pages from the text and send the remainder up to site. This is an example of why customs clearance can be slow in India! We hope something similar hasn't happened to our shipments.

## Slides of Europe

When we were in Bombay, Bill put in two rolls of slide film to Kodak, Bombay. They arrived by mail the other day. They turned out very well. When we get our sea shipment with our tape recorder we will make up a taped commentary and send both slides and tape back to "do the rounds" in Canada. India does not process Super 8 film and so far we have had conflicting stories about mailing it in or out of the country. As soon as we know of a safe method we will send the movie film to Canada for processing.

## Activities in the Township

There are a good number of social activities in the township. As well as badminton, tennis and table tennis, and the swimming pool (still not open!) there is a Friday night Square Dance club which we have enjoyed the past two Friday nights. A similar square dance club is planned for the children after school during the week. The adult class is a lot of fun with Canadians and some Indians learning Square Dancing from instruction tapes at the community centre. It's difficult for the Canadians, but pity the poor Indians who have never even seen Square Dancing before trying to keep track of the calls when English is their second language! To add to the confusion there are funny coincidences in the language. Last night an Indian remarked to Bill that in Hindi, "do-si-do" means "give me a pancake". How about trying to dance to that?

The children attended an interdenominational Sunday School for Canadian children at the school last Sunday. This Sunday, Margaret begins as a teacher. Most families in the community seem to be Catholic, but the organizer of the Sunday School, Mrs. W-- (the primary school teacher) is Baptist so she and Margaret will get along very well. Most children seem happy to go to Sunday School for a special activity on Sunday. When the swimming pool is closed they seem glad for any excuse for a change.

## A Walk Around the Site

With no car we have had a number of interesting walks around the site. On Thursday, after supper Bill and the children walked along a road leading toward the south-west of site and within a few minutes came upon a typical, small Indian settlement. The houses varied from simple one-room lean-to's made of scrub wood to stone houses with electricity. As we stood on the road you could see chickens, cows, water buffalo, pigs (Indian pigs look like wild boars without the tusks), sheep, goats, babies crying, and children waving and people sitting around eating, listening to transistor radios, working, etc. etc. It was a real experience. Bill can't wait to get some movie film and go back to let you see what it looked like for yourself.

Living here is much like living in a small rural community. On the way to school each day (a five-minute walk) we pass cows, dogs, goats and a variety of smaller wild life. There is an unbelievable variety of insects at this time of year. The children's favourite is a beetle they call an "Irving". It's really a rhinoceros beetle[7] - black, over 2 inches long with a small rhinoceros-like horn on its head. A quick check near the light in the garage any night will reveal at least a dozen different kinds of moths - some large and very pretty. We've also seen "walking stick" insects, many types of butterflies, wasps, hornets, beetles and flying bugs of all descriptions. The house is supposed to be bug-proof but it isn't really so the sweeper has a fair job each morning just getting them all cleaned up.

Snakes, scorpions, rats, Ginger spiders[8], etc. are just seen often enough by people in the community to take precautions such as checking your shoes, clothing and bedding, etc. - worthwhile at least for peace of mind. However, you adjust to the conditions surprisingly quickly. The children think it's great to see so many new and interesting kinds of life. There are many varieties of birds here too. It will be great when the binoculars come.

## Our First Souvenir

We bought our first Indian handicrafts the other day. A lady artist was down to the site from Delhi. She displayed some of her watercolour paintings and we bought two. One depicts an Indian workman helping his two oxen over a steep grade as they pull a typical old Indian two-wheeled cart piled high with goods. The other is a typical scene of an Indian vegetable market. They measure about 15 x 20 in. each and are pleasing at least to our artistically naive eyes.

## Indian Food

We have eaten very well since we came here. Fruits and vegetables are cheap and tasty. Meat is more expensive and some typically western food are not worth considering. For example - a small can of hot dog wieners cost over a dollar (7½ rupees)[9]. We have eaten papaya, pork, buffalo meat, prawns, Indian lentil soup (really

---

7    My recollection was that we used this name for a different insect, a Giant Water Bug.

8    This was the name commonly used for a supposedly venomous spider but we never found out what species it actually was.

tasty), and a variety of fruits and vegetables that are available locally including apples, plums, pears, potatoes, carrots, beans, etc.

The local store caters to Canadians and sells Coke, Fanta Orange, bubble gum, chocolate bars, candies, nuts, etc. Coke is about 7¢ a bottle (small size) with no deposit on the bottle but a promise to return it. The store-keepers can get pretty upset if you don't return them since the supply of bottles is limited and if you don't take them back the supplier won't sell the store-keeper more when stocks get low.

## Margaret Goes to Kota

Last week Margaret joined several of the ladies for a shopping trip to Kota (the nearest city). She went more as a sight-seer than as a shopper but it was an interesting experience. Kota sells almost anything you might want to buy IF you can find it. Many of the shops are crowded on narrow streets open to the street. You just go up one big step to get into them. Although the outside looks pretty bad, the inside often has a stock of goods not very different than you would expect to find anywhere else.

The rich Canadians get unbelievably good service. The women went into a number of material shops where they were given the full treatment. If anyone expressed the slightest interest in a bolt of materials then any others remotely similar would be taken down and thrown out across the length of the counter. They visited five stores and in each they left a pile of material almost 2 feet high and the full length of the counter (10 ft.) It must have taken the store-keeper's poor assistants ages to clear up after a visit. The women also were served free Cokes in every store. The main difficulty in every store was to get them to stop showing their wares and make up the bill so you could leave. As a result shopping can be very time-consuming but very interesting in India.

The worst part of Kota was the road between the stores. It was a narrow, muddy dirt road crowded with cows, goats, beggars, bicyclists, merchants with hand-carts, children and a few cars. Of course all roads in Kota aren't like this. The newer outskirts of the city are much better, but that isn't where the market is. If you can stand the smell, the dirt and the noise, the store-keepers are really nice and you can get some really good deals.

## Apologies

Our apologies for the poor copies on this letter. Once our sea shipment arrives, they will be dittoed off and much easier to read. In the mean time, write often. We like to get news from home.

---

9  Note that conversions between Indian Rupees and Canadian Dollars are those that were in effect when these letters were written: about 7½ Rupees to the dollar. By comparison, as I write this in 2023 the exchange rate was about 60 Rupees to the Canadian Dollar!

Our Fortunate Subscribers:

In case you were wondering, the following people receive copies of this illustrious document: Mr. & Mrs C. T--, Mrs. C. J--, Mr. & Mrs. R.H. O--, Mrs. & Mr. T.P. W--, Mr. & Mrs. J.D. J--. A further letter to other members of the families will be instituted when duplicating equipment arrives at the school.

Weather:

We are experiencing "monsoon" weather now - the worst time of year many people tell us. The rain really isn't too bad. Usually it's clear first thing in the morning then there are showers or rainstorms throughout the day interspersed with periods of sunshine. The rain comes very quickly when it comes. You can get caught 100 yards from a building and get soaked, but it's warm and not too uncomfortable. The rain leaks in everything. The walls of the house get very damp, during heavy rainfalls there are drips from the ceiling (we put pails on the floor if it gets too bad). The school is the worst. One day last week Bill had a puddle six feet across in one part of the school. All people look forward to the end of the monsoon but they appreciate this one time of the year when everything is lovely and green and growing unbelievably quickly. The temperature is in the eighties and nineties and the humidity is often 100%.

Time Zones:

There have been several questions about time zones and relative time between here and Toronto. We are ten and a half hours later than Toronto. Therefore if it is 9:00 p.m. here (which it is) then it is 10:30 a.m. on the same date in Toronto. This gets rather confusing because we get the sun before you since the earth travels from west to east and we are further east than you. Note: since the earth travels from west to east, this gives the impression of the sun travelling from east to west. We are further east than you so we get the sun sooner and our time gets later earlier than yours does. Right? Now I bet you're really confused.

Air and Sea Shipments:

We mentioned that we were existing on our travel luggage in our last letter. Things have improved somewhat. We have received our first air freight and half of our sea shipment. Things were in pretty good shape although some of the sea shipment was soaking wet from the trucking from Bombay to Kota during monsoon rains. The boys had their walkie-talkies confiscated in the air freight shipment. They are illegal in India without special permission and a permit so we may attempt to get permission. The red tape will be tremendous, but it will make an interesting hobby to write all the necessary letters and fill out the required forms. India is famous for those! We are reasonably comfortable now with our freezer, our washing machine (minus the wringer – it's in the other half of the shipment, with our clothing, bedding, food, frying pan, etc.) We look forward to the rest of the order any day now.

## Films:

Everyone says that it is almost impossible to get Super 8 movies out of India but we are going to try. Tomorrow we are sending two rolls of Super 8 film taken last Saturday in and around the township. It includes shots of our house, yard, school, playground and the community. It will give you a good idea of what RAPP Township looks like IF it gets through. Apparently many movie films are stolen in the mails before they leave India. If these films are stolen we shall use the alternative plan used by most Canadians – retake the films and send them out with the first Canadian leaving India on a visit, holiday, etc. This isn't too difficult to do and does ensure delivery of the films. The films will be sent to Mr. T--. Then they must be sent to Kodak for processing. I'll ask him to notify you if the films arrive and turn out all right so that you can get them for viewing.[10]

## Any Summer Catalogue Pages?

The Indian tailor in Rawat Bhata can make clothes from pictures such as those found in Eaton's and Simpson's catalogues. If you can, send pictures of attractive SUMMER clothes for women and children so that we can choose several and ask the tailor to make them up. Don't try to send a whole catalogue – it's too expensive. Just send several pages enclosed in a letter.

## Independence Day

Saturday, August 15th was Independence Day – a national holiday in India commemorating India's independence from Britain (achieved in 1947). There was a ceremony in the township park at 7:00 a.m. with the raising of the Indian flag. There were lots of speeches, newspaper articles and public gatherings throughout the country.

## Rakhri Day

Monday, August 17th is called Rakhri Day in India. It, too, is a holiday for many Indians (but not for the plant or the school!) In the morning Indian girls give a special decorated bracelet to the men of the family symbolizing good wishes for a safe and prosperous year. Acceptance of the Rakhri by the men is also a promise to protect the girl and provide help whenever needed. Rakhris are sold by the hundreds. They look like a small Christmas tree ornament on a string to tie it on your wrist. Rosan (Row-shann) our sweeper gave Bill a Rakhri first thing in the morning and gave Margaret and the children one around noon. The sweeper at the school also gave Bill one. With servants the accepted response is a small gift of money from the

---

10  The films indeed made it back to Canada. Years later I had some of them transferred to digital format and they can be found on YouTube here: https://tinyurl.com/2p9et9tt

employer. We followed the custom. Many of the children came to school wearing one or more Rakhris. It provided an interesting topic of discussion during the morning.

## Scorpions

This is the active time of the year for scorpions in the township. Last Friday, the gardener two doors away caught a 4-inch black scorpion in the garage. They put it in a jar and Bill took it to school for a lesson on scorpions on Monday. The poison from it was sufficient to cause serious illness or even death. On Sunday, David found a small scorpion in the upstairs bathroom. It was a two-inch white scorpion. Venom from this species is less dangerous. A sting is about the same as that of a hornet or wasp. We killed it with a fly swatter. Scorpions look like crabs except for their long jointed tail. However, they are arachnids - members of the same species as spiders, daddy-long-legs, ticks, mites, etc. The black scorpion Bill took to school was put in a jar of methyl hydrate to preserve it and show it to new pupils that come to the township.

You can be sure we check our beds, clothing and shoes before putting them anywhere near us at this time of year.

## Margaret's Shopping Adventures

In our last letter you heard the thrilling story of Margaret's trip to Kota. This week, she went to a small Indian village on the other side of the dam (called Phase 2 because it was built by the plant). While there with 3 other women and two teen-aged boys, the car broke down. After attempting to get it started (by hammering the starting relay in truly feminine fashion) they stopped several Atomic Energy jeeps and a truck. None however could get the car going fast enough to get it started (automatic transmission). Of course as they attempted to get it started they were surrounded by Indian children and other interested passers-by. Finally they went to the home of the wife of an Indian doctor at the local hospital. After further delays they were given a ride back to RAPP in the local ambulance leaving the poor woman who owned the car to wait for servicing of the car with her teen-aged sons. Their names were duly recorded in the ambulance driver's trip records. That will look rather strange when checked - if it ever is. All the women were disappointed however, for when they made their grand arrival in the ambulance no-one was around to see them. What a waste!

## The Local Hospital

Today Margaret joined several other ladies for a trip to the local hospital - purely as a sight-seer. The hospital is small, with narrow halls and very crowded (with Indians). The walls are dirty but the hospital is reasonably clean outside of that. It services all personnel on the project. Medical coverage is very inexpensive. Bill pays 27 rupees a month (less than four dollars) for complete medical, hospital coverage and all drugs for himself, the family and Mary, our cook. Margaret saw the hall where doctors have their individual offices. There was a long line of Indians before each office. The doorway is covered by a curtain and usually the first six people waiting were already in the room when someone was being examined, treated, etc. Not very much privacy. Canadians get privileges though. When they are noticed in line they are invited to come forward for examination or treatment right away. Several of the doctors are supposed to be excellent. Any Canadians who have undergone treatment, operations, etc. seem quite satisfied with the way they were treated but the surroundings take a bit of getting used to.

## Our Volkswagen Camping Van

While in Bombay we were notified that our van had been shipped and would arrive in Bombay toward the end of August. We plan to go down to Bombay the first week in September to pick up the car and do some shopping for school supplies, etc. After that we will be doing a lot more travelling than at present and should have lots of interesting things to tell about.

## We Feel Terrible!

So far we've received a number of letters but none have acknowledged the receipt of our letters. There is a delay of a week to ten days from the time they are sent until they arrive. We feel guilty when we read constant hints and suggestions that we write. We really are writing regularly – about once a week whenever possible. In fact we've already used two whole books of air mail paper. We hope you have at least one letter by the time we are writing this one. You certainly should have.

## Gift Packages

For your information the following suggestions should be followed to ensure that a gift package arrives. (Note: this is not a suggestion that you send a gift package!) Package should be marked with a total value less than five dollars – this includes postage – so underprice the contents and send only small things or the postage alone will be more than that. If you follow these instructions we will most likely get the package without paying duty on it. Since duty is often 100% of the value including postage this can be substantial. Note: This still doesn't guarantee that we'll get it but it certainly improves our chances.

## Closing Remarks

Everyone is healthy and happy. I think we are all going to gain weight if we're not careful. With a cook preparing all the meals, you seldom have a light snack just thrown together – the food is plentiful and tasty.

The weather does not bother us – there are lots of fans and air conditioned bedrooms. You only really notice it when you do some hard physical exercise outdoors – then you just drip with perspiration.

Bill played a tag game using scoops and balls outside the school for about 45 minutes tonight. He came home with every inch of his clothing soaking wet. You take lots of baths and showers and the amount of washing increases considerably. Still it's much like a combination rural town - summer resort as we hope you will see in our movie. (We're sending it air mail - registered so we've done everything we can to get it there safely).

All Bill's photographic equipment arrived including air mail weight photographic paper and enlarger so you can look for occasional black and white prints in future letters too.

Change of Address
Don't forget that change of address:      Mr. & Mrs. W. H. Tranter,
                                          H7/5,
                                          RAPP Township,
                                          Via Kota,
                                          Rajasthan, India.
Hoping to hear from you again soon!

                          Love to all,
                          Margaret, Bill, Jeff, Linda & David.

H7/5, RAPP Township,
Via Kota,
Rajasthan, India
August 29, 1970.

Dear J--, L-- & D--,

We got your letter of August 12th this week. Glad to hear everything's fine with your "addition-to-be". You and G-- are a real pair for combining reproduction with dieting. What is this - a new trend in motherhood?

It sounds like you had a good time on your holiday. You've probably noticed that holidays aren't the same even with one child, but they are satisfying in different sorts of ways. And they get better as the kids get older - unless you keep having more and more!

We got our freezer with the arrival of the first half of our sea shipment. It was in perfect condition so we were really pleased. So far we have been using it to store items that are not always available at the local store - like bread and butter, some of our imported Canadian foods like cake mixes, etc. (it keeps the bugs out), meat, vegetables, etc. It's great for making piles of ice cubes, popsicles, etc. Last week we froze our big five-gallon plastic jug and took it along to square dancing on Friday night. It was well received. It's unbelievable how fast ice melts around here though.

We were interested to hear you thought of going to England next year. You would enjoy it. We would have loved to go to other places outside of London too but we didn't have time. But there's lots to see and do and no problem adjusting like in most foreign countries. The only disadvantages we found in London were the cost - it is quite expensive - and the lack of good food. We didn't go to many decent restaurants but there was a poor selection in most places by Canadian standards. Sorry we won't volunteer to look after your kids even if you do agree to send them to India. Try someone without kids of their own. Maybe they'll be more naive!

A couple of hours ago the son of a neighbour two doors up brought us a nice fish to the door - one of two he caught this afternoon. It is a "Sand Felt" (?) It weighed about 3-4 pounds at least and was about two feet long. The other one he caught was even bigger. This fellow is an avid fisherman and catches decent fish almost every day. Bill is looking forward to getting the fishing tackle in the other half of the sea shipment. The river is teeming with fish. Very few Indians fish and those that do use rather primitive methods like thick green line, hook, sinker, and some type of dough bait.

Well, that's about all for now. We're enclosing another newsletter. We hope you're enjoying them. Write soon. We appreciate the news from home.

Love,
Bill, Marg, Jeff, Linda, David.

August 29th, 1970

Well it's Saturday night, 9:00 p.m. The nearest K-Mart, drive-in movie and take-out restaurants are closed. Even if they weren't, they're over a thousand miles away so we've decided to write another newsletter. (Actually it's one of the few nights this week we've been in. Mary, our cook, has acted as chief baby-sitter three nights this week!)

## News About the Children

Several people have mentioned that they haven't heard much about the children. They are enjoying their stay in India very much. They have loads of children to play with - more friends really than they had in Canada. As well as attending school the boys spend hours hunting for "bugs" - there are lots of big ones here - playing "catch", soccer, flying paper airplanes, exploring, visiting the recreation hall for ping pong and badminton and generally just hanging around. Linda plays skipping, visits other girls and does most of the things she would do at home.

On Tuesday nights there is square dancing for the children after school (Linda and David go, but Jeff won't). At present applications have been sent for cubs and brownies (*bulbuls* in India) to the nearby Indian scout troop in Rawat Bhata. If they won't accept the applications we'll start our own packs in Township, but we're hoping Canadians will be welcome there too. The kids in township don't seem to miss television very much. They are probably more active and read more than children in Canada. They all certainly look healthy.

## Sea Shipment and Car

We still don't have the second half of our sea shipment. We haven't seen it now for five months! This week Bill started to put pressure on D.A.E. in Bombay with cables, letters, and a talk with the Project Chief here at site. We expect action very soon. The car should arrive in Bombay within three days. We should have it in less than two weeks.

## School News

School has been in session four weeks now. The children seem to be enjoying it. The basic routines have been established and a number of "special events" have been started. Last Friday, Bill's class had their first "assembly". The Grades 5-8 pupils presented several skits and songs in a 20-minute presentation to the Grades 1-4 pupils. Mothers were invited. They all thought it was just wonderful. Since there is no auditorium, the assembly is held in the open central courtyard of the school. It was rained out in the morning but our luck held in the afternoon and the assembly was completed just minutes before another downpour!

Another big event is the paper airplane contest scheduled for Monday afternoon. Almost every child in the school is signed up to participate in two categories of distance and duration. Bill purchased the prizes in Kota - two little metal trophy cups for each class.

The grade 7's and 8's have begun work on a school magazine called the "Rapptrap Journal". It will include stories, poems, jokes, cartoons, etc., etc. by pupils in the school. We'll send you a copy when it's published.

There are now about 38 pupils in the school with five more large families expected within two weeks. Then the school should be up close to its maximum number.

All our own kids are enjoying school and progressing well. David can read quite a few words. Linda is doing well and really likes her teacher (so does David!). Jeff doesn't seem to have had any difficulty adjusting to having his father for a teacher. He is working well and enjoying school.

## A Snake!

Did you know snakes can climb stone walls? Margaret does. She found one on the window sill of our second-floor bathroom this week! At first she just saw the tail and thought it was a gecko (lizard) but when she moved the window she saw more of the body. She closed the door of the bathroom and went and got the gardener from next door to come up and kill it since no-one else was home in our house. The snake was a 2-ft. long Wolf Snake - non-poisonous, but similar in appearance to the Banded Krait which is highly poisonous. (Correction: Margaret tells me it was the cook from two doors away that killed the snake and not the gardener - Ed's note.)

## Extra Classes

The RAPP Township Sunday School is going strong with five teachers and about 35 kids attending each week. Margaret teaches Grade 3-4 level girls and boys. Most children who attend the school go to the non-denominational Sunday School. It goes from 10:30 until 11:30 a.m. on Sundays at the school.

Wednesday nights are Hindi Lesson nights for us. Mr. K--, husband of the school librarian, teaches a few interested Canadians. At present we are still working on the Hindi alphabet and doing some conversational work. The sounds of the alphabet are tough. There are over 40 different letters - some with sounds that are practically indistinguishable to Canadians. With luck though, it is possible that we would be able to speak a little bit of Hindi in 6 months or so. When we know a little more we'll give you some sample words written in Hindi.

## Accident In Township

There was a very unfortunate accident in the Township a few days ago. Two of the teen-aged boys were playing with gunpowder. While putting the gunpowder in a piece of copper tubing, the gunpowder exploded seriously injuring the left hand of a 17-year-old. He was rushed to the hospital where he underwent surgery almost immediately. He lost parts of at least 3 fingers and some bone from his hand. They asked for volunteer blood donors but they were not needed. The boy is recovering, but how much use he will have in that hand is not known. The parents were very concerned of course. The two boys were known for going off doing "experiments" all the time. Both boys feel very badly about their foolish behaviour as you can imagine.

## Shopping In India

"I never thought I'd be shopping in places like these when I was in Canada" was Margaret's comment today after we borrowed a neighbour's land rover and drove into Rawat Bhata. The stores are little more than open-fronted shacks with racks to display the produce. In spite of their small size and limited quantities of stock they usually have quite a variety of vegetables, fruits, etc. for sale. Canadians get the "royal treatment" - always served first and given special privileges such as being invited to come around the back of the store and inspect the rest of the stock. There are very good prices on some items. Bananas cost about 1 rupee (15¢) a dozen. Eggs are 4 rupees (60¢) a dozen. Items not easily available in the area can be very expensive. Our local store recently was trying to sell 7-lb. cans of prunes at about 110 rupees. In case your math is weak today that's about $16.50. Our food bill for a month is close to 2,000 rupees ($300.00). As well as that there are other expenses like $40.00 for electricity for a month. Since my living allowance is only about 2,000 rupees you can see that we can't live on that alone.

We wonder how the Indians in the community ever survive. Their total pay is only a fraction of Bill's total salary and they must pay income tax, school tuition fees, rent on their homes, appliances, etc. as well as even higher rates for things like electricity (our rate is subsidized!). No wonder most Indians live in little shacks. The top engineers on the project must have difficulty making ends meet living in the RAPP township.

## An Indian Bank Account

I am sure you will be pleased to know that we now have a savings account with the State Bank of Bikaner and Jaipur in Rawat Bhata. It was established to avoid the inconvenience of having to go out to plant site to collect the living allowance each month (it's a ten-mile drive). The bank building is a stone building with a corrugated iron roof. Outside it looked pretty crummy, but inside it wasn't too much different than a Canadian bank. Bill was told that it would take several hours to get through all the "red tape" of opening an account but it only took 20 minutes. The letter of reference from our Canadian bank probably helped a lot.

## Monsoon Weather

Are you still wondering about monsoon weather? We've been having it for the last two weeks. It doesn't rain all the time but there are heavy rains usually several times a day lasting from a few minutes to a few hours. The rain comes up very quickly. You can get drenched in no time. When you look across the valley from our house you can sometimes see the rain travelling towards you right up to your own back yard! A typical picture of Bill going to school in monsoon would be wearing sun glasses, but carrying an umbrella. He often uses both several times in the same day.

## Door-to-Door Salesmen

What do you do when a salesman comes to your door in Canada? If you're like us, you close the door in his face. It's a little different in India. You can buy an unbelievable variety of things at the door including: rugs, brass work, hand embroidered table cloths, eggs, milk, fish, live chickens (killed to order) and black market money. Some of the salesmen are very reputable and can give you a real bargain. They'll come into your home and spend an hour or more showing you handicrafts. Some of the goods are really beautiful and reasonably priced by Canadian standards.

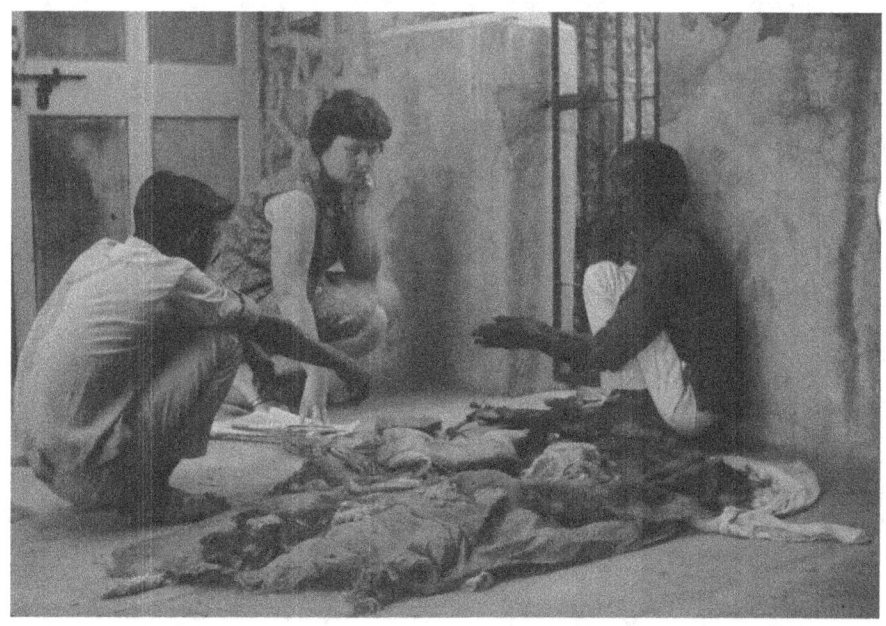

## Walk to Saddle Dam

Today Bill took David, Jeff and two other neighbourhood boys on a hike to Saddle Dam. It is about 3 miles away. Saddle Dam holds back part of the water in the reservoir near the township. There is a guest house there which is often used for parties, celebrations, meetings, etc. by groups of Indians. The boys and Bill walked across the dam and another half mile up a hill on the other side to a look-out tower on top of the hill which afforded an excellent view of the whole area for about ten miles around. On the way back across the dam it began to rain hard so they all ran for shelter to the guest house.

There they were greeted by a friendly and curious Indian. After a few minutes conversation in which the Indian found out that Bill was the local RAPP school teacher he discovered that the meeting being held there today was a teachers' group from Kota. So he was introduced to the local superintendent of education and some of the teachers. They were given a ride back to township on the teachers' chartered bus which was passing through RAPP on its way to Kota. So the hike turned out to be a very interesting experience for Bill and the boys.

## Any News?

Shame on all our relatives for writing such short letters! Any news from home is welcome. Indian newspapers give very little foreign news and almost nothing about Canada. Send along any news clippings of special interest. Let us known anything about Toronto or the rest of Canada that you think we might want to know.

Newspaper delivery here is rather erratic. Some days we don't get a paper. Then the next day we might get two. There is supposed to be a weekend magazine supplement with our paper. It was three weeks before we got one. The only consolation is the cost of the papers. The Times of India costs 18 paise per copy. It costs about $1.25 per month for the regular paper seven days a week plus the Sunday magazine supplement. I guess at those prices we can't complain.

## Pictures

Bill is still finishing up his first roll of black and white film. When it is developed, we'll send you some shots of our house, the township, etc.

We hope you get the movie we sent. If not, we'll make other arrangements another time.

The same problems getting film out of India seem to apply to tape recordings as well, but we'll try one of those when we get the tape recorders in our sea shipment and school supply shipment. Both of these are expected next week.

## In Case You're Wondering

Bill started typing this at 9:00 p.m. It's now 20 minutes to 11:00. The newsletters will still require covering letters, envelopes, addresses, a trip to the post office, etc. This letter-writing really is time-consuming. By the way, recent letters from Canada have taken close to two weeks to get through the mails so don't be surprised if our answers are slow too.

PLEASE WRITE SOON. WE ENJOY GETTING LETTERS. MARY, OUR COOK, GETS MORE LETTERS THAN WE DO AND SHE LIVES IN BOMBAY - NOT CANADA. SHAPE UP THERE!

Love to all from,
Marg, Bill, Jeff, Linda, David

Aug 30/70

H7/5
RAPP Township
Via Kota
Rajasthan, India

Dear G--, P--, S-- & G--,

Here is the next instalment in our continuing newsletter.   We received your letter dated Aug 10 on Aug 26 so by the time you get answers to your questions almost a month will have passed. There is no problem with stamps being removed from letters from Canada. People want stamps to use them not to save them so cancelled stamps are no good. The post office here cancels the stamps on our letters to you while we watch so that stops any problem of them being taken off.

We are eating very well here. Our township stores sell almost anything we need but really no choice of in case brands and the canned foods are of much lower quality than in Canada. The meats available are chicken, bacon, water buffalo, pork and lamb with goat available in Rawat Bhata cut up while you watch. We haven't tried it yet but we will. We eat Canadian type meals most of the time with an Indian meal about once a week.

We hope that by the time you get this letter we will have the rest of our sea shipment and maybe our van also. The ship carrying our van is supposed to arrive in Bombay any day now and we will be notified when to go down to get it. Bill & I will take the overnight train to Bombay and do some shopping while we are there. Then it will take 2 days to drive home.

Mary, our cook, used to be an ayah (nursemaid) and she is very good with the kids so we will be able to leave them at home.

Well let's see you write a nice long letter although I know you haven't got as much free time as I have.

Bye for now.

Love Bill & Marg, Jeff, Linda, David.

Sept. 7/70

Dear G-- & P--

Merry Christmas! I hope this package reaches you in time for Christmas. The tablecloth and napkins for G-- are an example of hand embroidery done in the Calcutta[11] area. The brassware is seen all over India of course. We thought the little water-pipe would be an amusing conversation piece. We will certainly be missing you at this time of year more than any other.

Love to all,

Bill & Marg
Jeff, Linda & David.

---

11  Now known as Kolkata.

Dear J--, L--, D-- and ?,

Along with the newsletter I'm enclosing several pictures from our first roll of b.&w. film developed in the township. I thought you might like a little explanation of each. They are numbered on the reverse side for easy reference.

#1 was taken from the balcony of the house so you can see we have a nice view. The water in the background is the reservoir that was formed when the dam was built right next to the RAPP Township. Under that stretch of water are some thirteen Indian villages and several old temples – all evacuated well before the waters came of course! The houses you see are much like ours. The streets are nicely laid out and there are trees planted along the sides and in some people's yards.

#2 is one of my favourite pictures. It is an Indian milkman delivering his wares. The brass pots carry his milk. All of the milkmen wear red turbans and ride bicycles. They deliver milk all day. This picture was taken outside of RAPP Township on the way to another nearby dam called "Saddle Dam".

    #3[12] is a typical monsoon picture. Linda and David had their rain
coats and an umbrella so I stood in our carport and took this
picture. They are not always so fortunate. Often they are caught at
school without a rain coat or umbrella. My monsoon equipment includes
sun glasses and an umbrella almost every day on the way to and from
school. When the rain comes up it comes up fast. The top soil is very
thin and roads, sidewalks, etc. flood within a few minutes and dry up
very quickly too.
    Each member of the family received a different selection of
pictures so check up with the others and you'll see some more points
of interest in RAPP township.
    I was glad to hear that you got the cheque I sent you. I was a
little worried because of the stories I've heard about Indian mail.
Have you received any of our mail opened or tampered with at all?
Have you heard anything about the films I sent about a month ago? I
hope they got through but I have my doubts. If my father got them he
should have let you know by now.
    Well Margaret says she has nothing to add so that's all for now.
Keep writing - you aren't doing very well so far!

            Love from,

            Marg, Bill, Jeff, Linda and David.

_____

12  Lost, unfortunately.

Dear G--, P--, S-- and G--,

Just a note to explain some of the pictures I am enclosing in this letter. My first roll of film in Township turned out pretty well so I'm sending you several shots. I've numbered the backs so you know which one I'm describing.

#1 is a picture I took several weeks ago on the way home from school. I had my umbrella and my camera. I was absolutely soaked to the skin so I said to myself "I should take a picture of this so people can see what a monsoon rain is really like". Unfortunately it doesn't show up as well as reality but I guess you can see that even after a few minutes the roads and sidewalks are covered with water and the ditches fill up quickly. Those are Indian homes something like small apartment buildings in the central part of RAPP Township.

#2 P--, before I came to India I was talking to a secondary school geography teacher who said he would dearly love to come to India to study the geography and particularly the geology of the country because it was fascinating. These rock formations are along the banks of the Chambal river. This river has dug out some of the most interesting formations over the centuries. Now because of the dam further up the river it is only about half its usual depth – which is still considerable but you can see an unbelievable expanse of naturally sculpted rock. Most of it is quite smooth and easy to walk

on. It's probably a great place for snakes too although I haven't
seen any yet.

#3 is at least a small proof that there really are cows in India.
David tried to walk up close to these young ones but they didn't
trust him and they got up off the middle of the road and moved on.
Notice the umbrella in case of monsoon. You never know when it will
come up next!

Margaret says she has nothing to add now, so just a reminder to keep writing. So far you haven't earned your newsletters! We look forward to your letters.

Love from us all,

Marg, Bill, Jeff, Linda and David.

Sea Shipment and Car News

Did you notice the difference in the type? This is the first newsletter typed on our own typewriter (a new one I bought for inclusion in the sea shipment). Our second half of the sea shipment arrived on Thursday evening around 5:00 p.m. We were getting pretty angry about the delay in getting it up here from Bombay so we were really pleased when we found that everything (or almost everything) arrived in good shape.

The only serious casualty was Jeffrey's guitar (an old one I fixed for him before we left). It arrived in about 7 pieces. The back was entirely off. The insides were rattling around in the box. The dampness must have loosened the old glue and it just fell apart. Bill's new guitar arrived safely as did everything else.

It was obvious that Indian customs had had a good look at most of the shipment. They are pretty careless in their repacking. Bill's new typewriter which left Canada packed in its original shipping carton consisting of: a case, a plastic bag, styrofoam packing in a cardboard box, arrived upside down in the case minus the styrofoam packing and the plastic protective bag. It didn't get wet however, so it wasn't damaged.

Thursday night and Friday were just like Christmas. Bill was pleased to get his guitar, typewriter, recorders, organ music, fishing tackle and tools. Margaret was happy to get her own kitchen utensils, bedding, cookware, new Melmac dinnerware and stainless steel flatware and electric appliances (blender, kettle, mixer, etc.) The kids were thrilled to see most of their toys. There has been a constant stream of kids in our house ever since playing Linda's games and bugging Jeff and David to get out their Eldon Touch Command cards, etc.

Rosan, our sweeper, and Mary, our cook, certainly had an interesting day on Friday looking at all the new stuff. At lunch time we noticed them both peeking out of the kitchen watching Jeff and David play with their remote control cars.

We must admit that we felt rather guilty on Thursday night. Here we are in a country where many people living within a mile of us live in wooden shacks with just enough money to eke out a bare existence and here we are with so many material possessions that we don't have room in our house to store them all.

We still don't have our car. Word is that it is likely going to be unloaded next week (the ship has arrived in port but the cars don't come off right away.) Two other families in the Township have Volkswagen Vans on the same ship so we're going to try to go down to Bombay together and return to site in a caravan of three Volkswagen Vans (Two camping vans and one mini-bus). Roads between Bombay and Kota have been bad during the past week and a half. The slight delay in the ship's arrival just may give them time to get the roads back in shape.

## More About Jeff, Linda and David

Two weeks ago Bill had his first class assembly programme which was dutifully and enthusiastically attended by the doting mothers. Jeff recited part of a poem, sang several songs in the class choir. Last Friday Mrs. W-- (the other teacher) had her first assembly. Linda led the class in a song called "Silly Willy", sang with the Gr. 3 & 4 girls and participated in several other songs by the class choir. David sang songs too, but his starring role was his debut as the back end of a cow in a cowboy skit.

Jeff and Linda are now attending an Indian cub pack and Bulbul pack. Bulbuls are Indian brownies. They are named after the Indian bird of the same name which is very common around here. The packs meet very regularly on Wednesdays from 3:30-4:30, Fridays from 3:30 to 4:30 and on Sundays from 8:30 to 10:30 a.m. They have ordered their accessories and will soon get their Indian uniforms. Since the packs are Indian they are getting to meet a number of Indian children from the township. The meetings are held in Phase 2 which is a settlement about 2-3 miles away across the dam. Fortunately there are some other Canadian children attending so that they can get a ride until our car comes. The meetings are in English but some of the songs are in Hindi, so that it should be a really good experience for them.

## Ganesh Chaturthi

In case you're wondering "Ganesh Chaturthi" is an Indian holiday celebrated by Hindus mainly from the state of Maharashtra (that's where Bombay is!) on September 4th. "Ganesh" is the Hindu god of wisdom and is often symbolized by an elephant. On the morning of the holiday the chief project officer for RAPP invited some Canadians to his house to see the service which he conducts for this holiday. He is a Brahmin (highest caste in Hindu culture). Bill had just started out on a long hike with the kids but Marg was invited to go with some other Canadians.

The service was conducted in front of a family altar decorated with leaves, corn, flowers and candles in the centre of which was a plastic statue of an elephant. The service in Hindi included prayers and praise to the god Ganesh and the giving of symbolic offerings of green leaves and food. The service was conducted by the man and his son and he stopped to explain the service to the Canadians as he did it. At the end of the service everyone threw in a handful of rice and flower petals. Then they ate the food offered to the god – an assortment of Indian sweets and delicacies.

The service was most interesting. Apparently he often invites Canadians on special occasions and we hope to be included again.

## Fishing

Since the fishing tackle arrived on Thursday Bill was eager to go out and try fishing. Today he was invited to go down to the river after supper with the man two doors up (an avid and regular fisherman). After fishing for about twenty minutes from the bank of the Chambal river Bill hooked and landed a 21½ inch, 4½ lb. Massur[13] (a fish similar to a carp in Canada). It gave quite a good fight and took 5-10 minutes to land. Later he caught a small trout as well. Since these were the only decent fish caught tonight he was quite pleased with his first Indian fishing trip. We are told that fishing tonight was poorer than usual. For example, last night the man up the street went fishing and caught 7 fish – 4 trout (very tasty eating) and three Massur (which most people usually give to the Indians to make curry since they are rather bony).

Canadians use fairly heavy nylon line, casting reels and spoons such as Red Devils, or plain silver coloured ones. Bill looks forward to more fish. The record Massur for a Canadian so far is ten pounds and <u>much</u> bigger ones have been hooked but not landed. Bill says that as far as fishing is concerned this is like being on summer holidays all year round!

## Photographic News

Bill developed his first roll of 35 m.m. b.&w. film the other night. It turned out pretty well. If you are one of the privileged few you will find several photographs included with this letter. More will follow as time goes on. Don't forget that you can send photos here too. We would like to see pictures of anything of interest with you too. If you like, just send negatives and we'll make our own prints!

## Letters to the Editor Column

Here is a new feature of our newsletter! Occasionally people have specific questions they want answered which would be of interest to all. This week, the prize-winning questions have been chosen and they are typed here with the answers.

R.H.O of Weston Ont. writes...
What are the sunsets like in India?
Answer: Sunsets are very beautiful at this time of year (during monsoon season). The cloud formations are extremely attractive and the sky has a beautiful red glow for about 15 minutes every evening. (Around 7:00 p.m.)

R.H.O of Weston writes...
When it is very hot there, is it clear or is it more misty like it is when it is hot here?
Answer: We are told that it is hazy during the hot weather. Since the average temperature in the past couple of weeks is around 85 degrees we can't tell. This is still the cool season.

---

13  The correct spelling is "Mahseer".

R.H.O. of Weston writes...
Does the cook prepare what you want for meals or does she plan them herself?
Answer: She generally plans them herself. Of course we can request anything we want. She was pleased to get our Canadian cook books so she'll likely be experimenting in the next couple of weeks.

Do you find the evenings drag and does Margaret get bored during the day time? (Another question by R.H.O. of Weston!)
Occasionally we do get bored during the evening. It will take a while to break the old evening t.v. habit. Most nights however, we find lots to do or visit other families or have company. Lots of social life around here! Now our hobbies have arrived too.
       The same kind of answer applies to Margaret. Occasionally a day drags, but most of the time there is someone dropping in for a visit or to invite her to go shopping somewhere. Things will be even better when we have the car. She can roar around all day running down cars, water buffaloes, bicycle riders, etc. between here and Kota.

PLEASE NOTE: The prize for sending in the best questions for the week is the top copy of the newsletter. No more eye strain reading rotten carbons! Of course the prize goes to R.H.O. of Weston. Next week it could be you!! That is, if you write us a letter.

An addendum from Margaret: The J-- family is not keeping up with the Tranter's in letter writing. Let's get going!

D.O. of Weston writes... Are you starting to get tanned?
Answer: Not much. We've had lots of cloudy days. When it's sunny it's too hot to stay in the sun for long. Most people here get their best tan during the cooler winter months.

Nobody asks... Is the pool open yet?
Answer: I'm glad you asked that question. No. But we hope it will open next week. They have started to clean it out.

"Wondering Senior Citizen" of Yorkdale Cres. writes...
How does the price of material in India compare with Canadian prices?
Answer: Cotton for dresses is 4-6 Rupees per Metre (about 75¢ for a little more than a yard) for 45 in. width material. There is a wide range of materials available in Kota and Rawat Bhata including: cotton, silk, nylon, plastic, suiting, drapery material, sari material, etc. You can buy dress lengths of material already embroidered for neckline and hem.

That's all for now. Write soon. Love to all from,
Margaret, Bill, Jeff, Linda and David.

Most of our newsletters so far have shown good things about India. This will be a real mixture of sad and happy news, so have your crying handkerchief and your laughter medicine handy. Here goes!

## News of the Car (Sad!)

You'll never guess that happened to our car. A few weeks ago we learned that our Volkswagen Van and two others were being shipped on the same ship and were due to arrive at the same time. We thought that was great because we could all (the 3 families) go down to Bombay together and drive back together. Then on Monday night we heard the news. The three cars were shipped together and they had been doing something else together throughout the whole voyage from West Germany to Bombay – namely – banging against each other. The cars had not been properly moored in the hold and it seems that the ship likely experienced a severe storm early in the voyage. The cars smashed into each other doing a great deal of damage. All three new Volkswagen vans (worth over $12,000.00) were in extremely damaged and rusted condition when they arrived in Bombay and guess which one was most damaged? That's right, ours! So, all three families have requested that the cars be replaced with three more brand new ones from West Germany. The insurance agents haven't agreed to do that yet but we hope they will very soon. So it looks like we'll be lucky to have a car by Christmas. Sob! Just so you can join us in a few tears here are some excerpts from the telegram received from Atomic Energy Personnel in Bombay who saw our car:

"Extensive damage to front half of vehicle through transverse crushing applied to front doors, worse on right side, involving front and centre doors, doorframes, front panel, possibly body surface and floors, wheel alignment, etc. Rust on scraped surfaces indicates significant time lapse since damage occurred."

This is particularly annoying when the nearest city is over 30 miles away and the car that was damaged has been paid for in full since last April! So please join us in a good cry!

## An Alternative

Realizing that our car is not likely to be available for at least 3 more months Bill has come up with an alternate form of transportation! Today Bill and Marg were in Kota with one of the other grieving Volkswagen owners looking at motorcycles! Bill and the other man have just about decided upon a Rajdoot Ranger each. This is a lovely, fairly powerful motorcycle – black and chrome coloured – 6 h.p. with leather seats and all accessories available for immediate

---

14 Newsletter #5 is either missing or was inadvertently skipped in the numbering of letters. I strongly suspect the latter, as only seven days had elapsed since the last newsletter.

delivery. This is Saturday and they were prepared to drive the motorcycle up for delivery on Monday, but the other man (and Bill) were both just a little short on the necessary cash needed for the purchase so they didn't buy it yet. Instead we will price them in Bombay on our trip there next week (see below for further details!) Anyhow, it is likely that by the time you get your next letter from us we will be the proud owners of a Rajdoot Ranger (costing Rs. 4,320.00). Soon there should be enough motorcycles in the Township to start the RAPP Rat Pack. Look for pictures of Bill in his black leather jacket and motorcycle boots. Also look for news articles of a Canadian teacher being killed after smashing his motorcycle into a sacred cow. (If the crash doesn't kill him the outraged Hindu witnesses will.)

We found out a few things as we shopped around that might interest you. First, in case we haven't mentioned it yet, you should know that Indian cities generally group stores that sell similar products in the same area. For example, in Bombay, there is one street that just sells electrical goods, another that sells material, etc. Kota is somewhat the same for motorcycles. We visited all the motorcycle and motor scooter dealers in the city today. We had a choice of three makes and about 6 models of Indian made motorcycles. All were in stock and immediate delivery for cash – time payments were never considered by dealers we spoke to. We went into the main motor scooter dealer too. He had about 12 models in the showroom – all the same. We asked about cost, guarantee, motor size, etc. and then after receiving some very interesting answers we were told that if we would like to buy one we could put our name on the waiting list. The dealer would call us when our scooter was ready in about four years. Yes – there is a four-year waiting list for motor scooters from motor scooter dealers. Now it is possible we were told to buy one on the "open market" – i.e. a private sale right away, but the cost was 1,000 rupees more than the quoted price. That made the motor scooter price just about the same as for the Rajdoot Ranger so we gave up on that! We were told that the waiting list for another more popular brand of imported motor scooter was 10 years!

This goes to show just how serious the problem of manufacturing complex articles such as cars and motor scooters is in India. There is a similarly long wait for automobiles of Indian make and imported vehicles are almost impossible to buy. India is terribly conscious of their foreign exchange in currency and hates to spend money on any imported goods that can be made in the country. Only special visitors – like the Canadians – are granted import licenses to bring cars into the country and then only on the understanding that we export them at the end of our stay. A used car – such as our Volkswagen – could be sold for considerably more than its new price after we used it for two years if we were allowed to sell it before leaving. We are allowed to sell our cars to other Canadians on the understanding that they in turn will export it back to Canada. This has some interesting consequences for one of our neighbours who bought a third-hand

Volkswagen Van from another Canadian. The car is on its last legs (or last wheels) and even if it's a total wreck it must be exported to Canada at the end of his stay unless he can sell it to another Canadian. If he does export it they'll never allow him to drive it on Canadian roads. It's all re-welded together and generally in rotten shape. Cars do not last well on Indian roads – they tend to be rather bumpy, servicing is poor and gas is not the best. The local gas station often has water in the gas. When it is clean it is India's regular 82 octane gas so you can imagine how a big engine would run on that. Thank goodness we didn't bring the Ford. It would have coughed itself to death on every hill with 82 octane gas (lowest in Canada is 100!)

By the way we went into Kota via D.A.E. (Dept. Of Atomic Energy) jeep. What a bone-jarring experience. The rat patrol never had to ride a wreck like that! However the cost was right. Probably about 40 rupees ($6.00) for a 70 mile round trip with car and driver included.

India's Garbage Collectors:

On the way to Kota we saw either a cow or water buffalo that had been the victim of a hit-and-run accident. It was obviously freshly killed. That was around 1:00 p.m. At 5:00 p.m. on our return we checked the same place and found just the remains of the carcass – even all the bones were gone and there were about 6 vultures just finishing off their feast. About ½ a ton of meat in four hours!

One sect in India[15] uses this method for the disposal of human bodies. I hear that it takes about 20 minutes for the vultures to pick clean a human skeleton offered up for "burial" by them.

The Swimming Pool (Good News)

Dry your tears of pity for the poor Tranters. As the Canadian weather gets cooler, India's monsoon is over and every day is hot and sunny with temperatures between 85 and 95 degrees. Just perfect for the newly opened Olympic size swimming pool in the township. We have been swimming six times in the last five days.

Pity the poor school teacher who doesn't come home for lunch. Instead he walks to the pool with his children – swims for half an hour in the cool, clear, blue water then has a picnic lunch at the pool edge before walking 500 yards back to the school. I hear it's getting colder back in Canada already. Cold? What does that word mean? It has something to do with wearing heavy clothes doesn't it? What was that white stuff that used to come down? Snew? What's snew? (Not much, what's snew with you?)

Anyway, the pool is lovely. We'll take some pictures of us jumping off one of the three diving boards so you can see how the poor Canadians suffer here helping out a depressed country. We really do suffer, you know. Sometimes you have to wait more than five minutes before your maid brings you a cold drink after you order it.

---

15  The Parsis of the Zoroastrian faith.

The kids love the pool as much as the adults. They would spend hours there every day. We think David overdid it a bit the first few days because he hasn't been well yesterday afternoon or today. He complained of headaches and thought he was going to be sick to his stomach once. His temperature went up to 101 for a while but by tonight he seems to be recovering.

Speaking of sickness, a 12 year old boy up the street has a mild case of paratyphoid. Our inoculations should still be a help in preventing that.

Our Trip to Bombay

Next Thursday afternoon Marg and Bill leave for a shopping trip to Bombay. While there we will purchase school supplies, check on the shipment of an order of school supplies from Canada and view the wreckage of the three Volkswagen Vans. When we first planned the trip we planned to leave Kota about 4:30 p.m. and arrive in Bombay about 8:30 a.m. However, since then we've heard that the train trip is still being rerouted because of monsoon damage to train crossings and the trip takes 30 hours. If that is still true next week it will be a rather long ride each way to say the least! Anyway, the school supplies are desperately needed and D.A.E. pays Bill's way for the train and our stay at the beautiful Taj Mahal Hotel again so it won't cost too much. If we take pictures of the car we'll send you one! Sob again!

Films:

We were really pleased to hear that our two rolls of movie film arrived in Canada safely. I hope by now you have seen them and have some idea of the place. We were told by absolutely everybody that films sent from India would be opened and stolen, etc. It looks as if, either we were very lucky, or the stories were greatly exaggerated. Everybody that advised us not to send them had never tried to send any themselves so we figured it was worth a try.

Now that we have our movie light, etc. we'll take another roll or two of the inside of our house and other features of the township like the swimming pool, the playground, inside the school, etc. On the trip to Bombay we'll take more colour slides. There are opportunities for films everywhere in this country. Yesterday a wild monkey was sitting in the fence 500 feet down the road from our house eating a leaf. On Monday, on another trip to Kota I saw dozens of wild monkeys, dozens of peacocks, and a lizard at least 2½ feet long. It really gets you after a while – here we are travelling along a road that looks like northern Ontario in the summer time and suddenly you see all these strange animals. One family even saw a tiger on the road coming in from Kota very early one morning. Another family saw a leopard. We'll have to take enough slides and movies to have about five Indian Night parties when we get home to Canada (if the tigers don't get us first!)

## A Strange Request:

Lots of funny things happen here. Last night we opened a new Coleman thermos that we unpacked and found leaking around the faucet. Bill discovered a defective rubber washer. So, the rubber washer, the inspection slip, and a one-page letter requesting a replacement was sent registered airmail today to Coleman in Canada. Imagine their surprise to find a registered air mail letter all the way from India to find a request for a replacement washer! (It was registered because unregistered mail does tend to get opened if it is bulky or contains unusual shaped objects. Registered mail isn't usually bothered.)

## Fishing News:

Bill went fishing again on Sunday night last week and caught another Massir (?) this time about 4½ lb. Just send lures as presents from now on. He only brought about 4 and they'll be gone in no time. Silver coloured spoons or red and white Red Devil lures are likely best. If sending them, mark the package "unsolicited gift" and be sure that the declared value – including the cost of postage – is less than $5.00. (For example, air mail postage of $4.10 – value of gift $.50 for a total of $4.60. The estimated value of the gift does not have to be too accurate.)

## Enclosures

There are two enclosures in this letter – attached to the back of this page. One is an article from a Hindi newspaper so that you can see what Hindi writing is like. The other is an example of my favourite classified ad in our Times of India paper. They are matrimonial ads in which parents advertise for prospective brides or grooms for their children of marriageable age. We thought you might be interested.

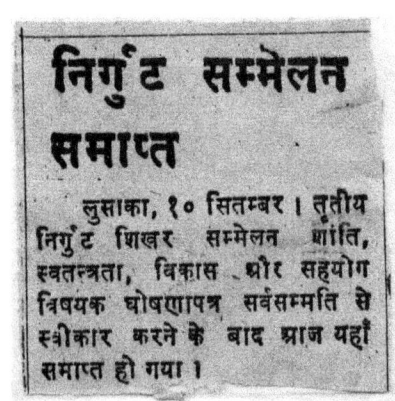

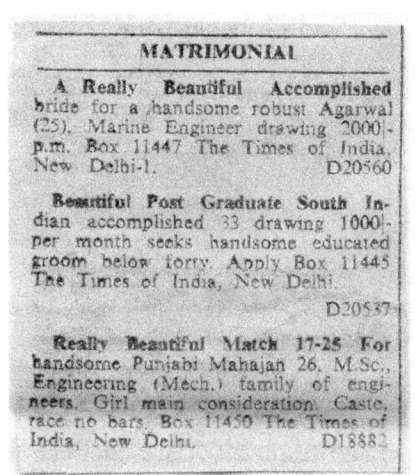

## Family Planning Fortnight

Did you know that Sept. 14th – 27th is Family Planning Fortnight in India? Every night there is an ad quoting some other well known Indian such as Indira Gandhi, Nehru, etc. on the importance of birth control. The weekend paper has a big article on the success of birth control ads in Bombay. Companies provide free time off for men to get sterilization operations and some offer bonuses of several hundred rupees as well.

Over-population is a serious problem in India in which 500 million people live in a country about 1/3 the size of Canada (pop. 20 million). There are several villages between township and Kota. Each has only one commercial road sign. It is written in Hindi and suggests to the local people that "two is enough". The Canadians are a terrible example. Most families here have 3 or 4 children. Some have five. If you were in India how would you celebrate "family planning fortnight"?

## This Week's Question Prize?

This week the prize-winning question came from several sources. It was "Did you get your car yet?" The prize is the last carbon copy of this letter soaked in tears. Hope you weren't the lucky winner!

Another prize-winning question comes from Bill Tranter who asks, "How come your family never writes, Margaret?" Although there is no prize for this we hope it will encourage more frequent letters from the J-- (G-- and P-- wrote this week).

## Margaret's Birthday

Margaret thanks you for the birthday cards she has received. She sends special thanks to those who did not mention that this was her 30th birthday. It's a good thing she has servants to help her now that she is a doddering old woman.

## Some New Possessions:

We are the proud owners of a genuine Indian rug - made in Kashmir. It is a small one - 4 ft. by 6 ft. but very nice and rather expensive. We also bought some Indian brassware. More about that again.

Love to all,

Bill, Marg, Jeff, Linda, & David.

## A Travelling Newsletter:

This letter is being written in unusual circumstances to say the least. Margaret and Bill are sitting in a 1st Class Air Conditioned Railway Coach approximately 200 miles north of Bombay on our return to Kota. We brought the typewriter so that Bill could get some school work done on the way down to Bombay. We brought airmail paper so that we could write our weekly newsletter on the way back. As you can imagine, the topics of this newsletter will deal with rail travel in India and the sights of Bombay revisited after two months.

## Rail Travel in India:

Because of the strong British influence for over 100 years, India has a well-developed railway system – the fourth largest in the world. Trains are dependable and generally inexpensive. The amount of luxury varies greatly with the class of ticket you purchase. For example, a third class sleeper – the usual way most Indians travel – costs about 35 rupees ($5.00) to travel one-way from Kota to Bombay, a distance of more than 750 miles. So far we haven't been able to discover what second class is, but there are also third class coaches (seats rather than bunks), first class compartments and air-conditioned first class compartments. Since that is the most comfortable way to travel long distances where cost is not a great concern, that's how we are travelling.

A.C.C. (first-class air-conditioned) compartments are quite nice. They include two beds (bunk style). The top one folds into the wall leaving a large and comfortable seat in the compartment – actually quite big enough for 4 people to sit on. There is a folding table, a cupboard big enough to hold most of the clothes you need for the trip, a wash basin with running water, a carpet on the floor, a fan in the ceiling, a large window, at least 6 different lights for general lighting, reading lights, night lights, a small mirrored medicine cabinet, 3 bells to ring for your porters, electrical outlet, a door – curtained for privacy and a louvred serving window for having the porter deliver items without opening the door.

There are also two full-time porters to serve 6 compartments. You can order cokes, food, complete meals, etc. For breakfast this morning we had a tray including: four boiled eggs, 4 slices of toast, a pot of tea, and 2 bananas. For lunch we have ordered: soup, mutton[16] cutlets, vegetables, coffee and fresh fruit – bananas and oranges. Food is very reasonable – on the way down, total cost for our breakfast, lunch and dinner was around 25 rupees ($3.00).

A.C.C. train fare, of course, is considerably more expensive than other classes. One-way fare for Margaret and Bill from Bombay to Kota is Rs. 482.00 (this is the usual way of writing rupees and paise in India). In Canadian dollars, that is a little less than $70.00 or

---

16  In India mutton refers to goat meat, whereas in most other countries it refers to sheep.

$35.00 each for one-way. This is higher than the usual A.C.C. rate because the usual Bombay-Kota route has been washed out by monsoon rains. Instead of spending fifteen hours on the train each way we spend 32 hrs. Indian Railways charge you more for this inconvenience!

Rail travel is an excellent way to see the countryside. We pass cities, towns, farmlands, hilly regions, rivers, reservoirs and all the usual Indian animals which you see wherever you go - cows, water buffalo, sheep, goats, chickens, etc.

Our trip began at around 8:00 p.m. last Thursday night with an hour's ride to Kota. Then a 2 hour wait at the station because the train was late. We boarded the train to Bombay at 11:45 p.m. Thurs. night and arrived in Bombay at 5:30 a.m. on Saturday morning where we were met by a D.A.E. car and driven to the Taj Mahal (hotel, that is). We left Bombay Monday night at 8:15 p.m. and hope to arrive in Kota Station around 2:00 a.m. on Wednesday morning. That's a lot of time to spend on a train, but it is comfortable and we brought books, school work, typewriter, etc. so that time passes quite quickly.

A Lucky Find:

The following incident happened on the way to Kota by D.A.E. jeep. It will show you why you seldom see litter on Indian roads.

About half way along the dark, deserted road from site to Kota the jeep's headlights picked up a dark sack in the middle of the road. It was obvious that it had been dropped from a passing car spilling vegetables and fruits on the road. Our driver swerved around it, then stopped and backed up the jeep. Then, with the jeep's headlights shining on the lost bundle he proceeded to get out and gather up all the spilled food - mainly potatoes and bananas, carefully pack them in the sack and bring them back to the jeep with a huge smile on his face. It was obvious that his family would eat well that night from his lucky find. And remember, this man is a permanently employed driver for the Department of Atomic Energy.

Fortunately he only spotted one such sack on the road that night or we would have never made it to the station.

Waiting at the Station:

Since the train was late we sat in the first-class waiting room - a common feature of all Indian railway stations of decent size. It was far from first-class! The seats were hard and poorly designed - much like wooden lawn chairs. The fluorescent lights in the ceiling attracted hundreds of insects through the open door, one waiting passenger slept on a wooden slatted bed provided in the room. Tea was served from a filthy pot by an old, shabby man who expected a tip whether you got tea or not. We had no tea, but we did meet an interesting Indian gentleman who spent the hour telling us about himself and his travels since his retirement from the Indian public service. He had occupied a fairly high position in the defence department, had studied in England and had travelled in many parts of the world. Since he wife died a year ago he has travelled by rail, air and ship to more places that interest him visiting family and friends and seeing the world. He loved to talk but seldom took time to listen. A sympathetic nod was all that was expected of us from time to time in return for his views on travel, politics, family history, etc. If you wish to contact him, we have his business card.

## Bombay:

Bombay seemed rather different this time than last time we were here. After two months without seeing a city any bigger or more westernized than Kota it looked much more attractive than it did on our arrival from a trip through Europe.

On the way in from the station we passed what must have been the main taxi terminal. At 5:30 a.m., the streets were deserted but along the side of a large square we saw literally hundreds and hundreds of Bombay taxis parked ready for the morning rush. They are all black and yellow cars – mostly Ambassadors – an Indian make of automobile with styling about 1948 in appearance. There are some Fiats and other vehicles as well but import restrictions on cars are so strict that relatively few imported cars can be seen. A 1961 Ford or Chevrolet occasionally seen looks like a real limousine. Jeeps are much more common than in Canada.

The Taj Mahal Hotel is still the ultimate in luxury with its beautiful rooms, icy air-conditioning and good service. Margaret and Bill had a fine opportunity to rest in luxurious surroundings in the morning we arrived before beginning a record-breaking shopping spree!

## School Supplies:

The first stop was for school supplies at Bombay Stationary Mart. Bill was greeted as a long lost friend because of the huge quantity of supplies he bought here in July. In just over two hours he spent almost Rs. 1,300.00 in the store (to get dollars, divide by 7). We bought duplicating paper, art paper, pencils, accessories, and on and on and on.

Then we went shopping for Indian reference books for the school. We bought about 40 different books of Indian nature study, legends and history for use in the school library plus another couple of dozen for ourselves. Contrary to what we heard before we left, good paperbacks are easily available and quite inexpensive. We get some titles before Canada does. You'll never guess what we saw in one store: A paperback copy of Al Boliska's world's worst jokes #2.

Every book store seem to have its little shelf of quasi-scientific sex books as well. Of course we completely ignored this section.

As we walked along the street – looking rather like tourists still, but not feeling like tourists, we were regularly approached by quiet little men who ask quietly if you wish to change American dollars. We must have been approached at least 2 dozen times during our stay in Bombay. They offer to exchange American currency – and in some cases even Travellers' Cheques at a rate of 10.2 rupees to the dollar instead of around 7 which is the bank rate. Then, of course, they sell this currency at a profit again to rich Indians, we suppose who wish to convert more of the rupees to dollars than the government will allow. Anyway, since we have no dollars we just laughed and told them we had only rupees.

From the hotel dining room window on Saturday morning we saw a snake charmer demonstrate his skills to a group of tourists and then offer to let his mongoose fight the snake. The usual procedure for these men is to get someone interested, then when they give him some money they invariably protest that it is not enough. If a tourist is foolish enough to agree to let him demonstrate his mongoose's skills in killing a cobra, then he will be expected to pay not only for the show but to replace the cobra (Cobra's are VERY expensive, Sahib!) so don't get caught in this trap if you come to India.

## An Excellent Dinner

Saturday night we dined at a restaurant that made us think we were back in Canada. Around 9:00 p.m. we arrived at Frederick's Chinese Restaurant and after a 5-minute wait we were seated. There are several good Chinese food restaurants in Bombay but this is often recommended as the best. We ordered sweet and sour chicken, a delicious shrimp, vegetable and noodle soup, pork and vegetable dish and fried rice and vegetable dish. The variety was much greater than most Canadian places. They offered as many as 20 different kinds of soup alone including exotic things such as shark's fin soup and many others. We had a delicious meal for a total cost of 36 rupees.

Margaret says that Indian Chinese food beats Canadian Chinese food any day!

## Sunday: A Trip to Elephanta Caves:

A few miles off the coast of Bombay there is an island (one of many) that was used as a monastery for the Hindu equivalent of monks in the 7th century. These monks used the natural cave formations and painstakingly carved out a series of temples for the worship of the Hindu gods. They are in pretty bad condition now because Portuguese sailors moored in the harbour several hundred years ago used to use the island as a good place to get roaring drunk and wrecked many of the abandoned stone carvings.

There is a ferry boat that caters to the tourist class leaving from the Gateway to India at 9:00 a.m. We had some trouble with a mix-up in our train tickets so we were unable to catch that boat. We had to go and exchange our tickets which were purchased for Sunday night instead of Monday night and the ticket office also opened at 9:00 a.m. We returned to the Gateway to India at 9:30 figuring we had missed out on our trip to Elephanta Caves only to find that a number of other ferry boats - designed for Indian patrons (slower, a little dirtier and noisier and much cheaper) were ready to leave so we bought the tickets at Rs. 3.50 each (instead of Rs. 12.00 for the regular tourist boat) and went. We were the only foreigners on the boat. The trip took about 1 hr. and 15 minutes to get to the island. We walked around for about 2½ hrs. This island is used for picnics by the Indians quite a bit and we saw a number of groups of Indians (generally fairly well-to-do ones) playing games, having contests, dances, singing, etc. It was our first real look at adult Indians at play. Since there were very few European tourists around we really got a good look at Indians being themselves unselfconsciously.

We observed a circle game somewhat like musical chairs in which Indian men change partners with the women, until the music stops and the one with no partner is out. We watched a stick dance in which all the girls were in a circle on the inside and the men in a circle facing them on the outside. The girls circle one way and the men the other in time to music played on a portable pump organ, drums, etc. and each dancer carries the rhythm of the music with two sticks which he or she hits against his partner's sticks and his own in an established pattern. Then the circle moves and they go to a new partner. The music gets faster and the rhythm harder to follow until finally they give up and berate the music makers for speeding up so much, but all in a good humour.

Some of the richest Indians hired porters to carry their picnic baskets and supplies. In one small picnic pavilion we saw utensils all laid out for a picnic lunch for a large group of people. At each place on the blanket covered floor there was a large banana leaf with a plastic cup on top, a sign of the unusual combination of old and new ways that you see so often in India. Much like this is the still strange sight of a heavy traffic jam on one street and a cart pulled by oxen on the next one!

## A "Cultural Experience"

Sunday evening we were invited to attend a concert of a double string quartet at the Indo-German Cultural Exchange House. The invitation came from the wife of an A.E.C.L. employee stationed in Bombay whom we met on our way in. She plays the cello in this group and invited us to attend the concert at 6:30 p.m. and come back for dinner at around 8:30 p.m. (Note: You can do this when you have servants - you should really get some - they're a big help!) The concert was quite good, attended by Indians, Germans and a mixture of others from teen-aged to retirement age. The double string quartet had Indian and German players. It is one of a number that are being encouraged to bring symphony orchestra experience to Bombay.

The dinner afterwards and the evening of conversation was most enjoyable.

## Our Poor Car

On Monday I went to Custom's House (Bill did) to see our car. It has not been cleared through customs and will probably be returned to Germany to be replaced by a new one. It is a terrible mess. Both sides at the front have giant slashes cutting right through the metal frame. The roof seems to have been pushed up out of shape by the pressure of the sides, the alignment is way out and at least one window is popping out of its frame. It would be close to impossible to repair. Estimates indicate the repairs would take at least 6 months so we hope they will work quickly on getting us a replacement.

## We Leave Bombay

On Monday night we left the hotel in a D.A.E. mini-bus and an unbelievable pile of parcels from personal and school shopping. We almost didn't get all the excess baggage arrangements made in time but with about two minutes to spare we had everything stowed on the train ready to go. The train left exactly on time so we were lucky we were ready.

Well that's all for now. Write soon,
Love, Marg & Bill & kids.

Thanksgiving Sunday:

We have just spent a quiet Thanksgiving Sunday. This morning the two older
children (you may remember them as Jeff and Linda)went to Indian cubs and
Bulbuls (from 8:30 to 10:30 a.m.) Then to Sunday School at 11:00 a.m. which
Margaret teaches. After lunch we went to the pool for a long afternoon
swim. Then, after a trip by Bill and David down to the store for squash
and cold beer on the motorcycle, we went out to supper at the White's house.
We ate chicken, scalloped potatoes, peas, tossed salad, baked potatoes,
jellied fruit salads, etc. and a choice of pumpkin pie or angel food cake
for dessert. So you can see, that we have lots to be thankful for on
Thanksgiving in India.
    By the way, the last two weeks in a row have been four-day weeks with
Mathatma Ghandi's birthday celebrated 2 Fridays ago and the Indian Harvest
Festival called Dusshera last Friday. Bill doesn't know how he is going to
manage a full five-day week. And there are no more holidays until Diwali
at the end of October!

The Motorcycle:

Did you notice the mention of the motorcycle. We now own a 9 H.P. Rajdoot
Ranger motorcycle. It is black with lots of chrome trim, has chrome leg
protectors on the front and two saddle baskets at the bag ample enough for
quite a decent amount of shopping. We have owned it for a week and half now.
It cost Rs. 4,200.00 and is quite decent for Bill and any other single
member of the family to ride on. We use it for shopping, trips to the local
village Rawat Bhata, going fishing, etc. It gets 30 Kilometres to the Litre
so you can see that the gas mileage is quite good! Pictures and more information
about the motorcycle will follow with later letters.

A Movie:

Last Saturday Bill and another RAPP resident went into Kota on their motorcycles
to get some srvicing done - just as with new cars in Canada, there are always
a few minor things wrong. While he was there he took a roll and a half of
colour movie film of the city of Kota. It is really something (if it turns
out). It will be mailed at the same time these letters are, so be ready for
notification of the next showing. It will be sent to Mr. Tranter again.
The final half a reel shows the Township swimming pool in full operation.
It's really most enjoyable - of course the weather is rather warm - every day
sunny all day with temperatures in the 80's and 90's. The weather is rather
boring really. You always know it is going to be bright, sunny and warm.
Very practical weather for swimming pools and motorcycles. By the way is
it getting chilly in Canada? Do you often go swimming these days? Or is the
weather already too chilly? It's hard to remember when you've been here as
long as we have.

Another Trip Into Kota

Margaret and Bill have a first in the township! On Saturday, October 10th,
they left the kids with a neighbour and went into Kota by motorcycle. (Two
people on one motorcycle of course!) The round trip is well over 100 Kilometres
(around 65-70 miles?) so it was quite an accomplishment. Besides buying some
things Margaret got a fine sunburn on her face, neck and lower lip and both
Bill and Margaret were stiff at the other end for several hours on their return.
But we saw some interesting things:
(a) Animals:

    As well as threading ourselves through the usual herds of cattles, water
buffalo, goats and sheep, we stopped within several feet of monkeys, saw a
a lizard about 2 feet long (including his tail) and ran over a snake. We almost
hit have a dozen vultures as they slowly took off the road in front of us as

64

Thanksgiving Sunday:

We have just spent a quiet Thanksgiving Sunday. This morning the two older children (you may remember them as Jeff and Linda) went to Indian cubs and Bulbuls (from 8:30 to 10:30 a.m.) Then went to Sunday School at 11:00 a.m. which Margaret teaches. After lunch we went to the pool for a long afternoon swim. Then, after a trip by Bill and David down to the store for squash[17] and cold beer on the motorcycle, we went to supper at the W--'s house. We ate chicken, scalloped potatoes, peas, tossed salad, baked potatoes, jellied fruit salads, etc. and a choice of pumpkin pie or angel food cake for dessert. So you can see, that we have lots to be thankful for on Thanksgiving in India.

By the way, the last two weeks in a row have been four-day weeks with Mahatma Gandhi's birthday celebrated 2 Fridays ago and the Indian Harvest Festival called Dusshera last Friday. Bill doesn't know how he is going to manage a full five-day week. And there are no more holidays until Diwali at the end of October!

The Motorcycle:

Did you notice the mention of the motorcycle? We now own a 9 H.P. Rajdoot Ranger motorcycle. It is black with lots of chrome trim, has chrome leg protectors on the front and two saddle baskets at the back ample enough for quite a decent amount of shopping. We have owned it for a week and a half now. It cost Rs. 4,200.00 and is quite decent for Bill and any other single member of the family to ride on. We use it for shopping, trips to the local village Rawat Bhata, going fishing, etc. It gets 30 Kilometres to the Litre so you can see that the gas mileage is quite good! Pictures and information about the motorcycle will follow with later letters.

A Movie:

Last Saturday Bill and another RAPP resident went into Kota on their motorcycles to get some servicing done - just as with new cars in Canada, there are always a few minor things wrong. While he was

---

17  Squash is a non-alcoholic concentrated syrup added to carbonated or still water to make a refreshing beverage.

there he took a roll and a half of colour movie film of the city of Kota. It is really something (if it turns out). It will be mailed at the same time these letters are, so be ready for notification of the next showing. It will be sent to Mr. T-- again. The final half a reel shows the Township swimming pool in full operation. It's really most enjoyable - of course the weather is rather warm - every day sunny all day with temperatures in the 80's and 90's. The weather is rather boring really. You always know it is going to be bright, sunny and warm. Very practical weather for swimming pools and motorcycles. By the way is it getting chilly in Canada? Do you often go swimming these days? Or is the weather already too chilly? It's hard to remember when you've been here as long as we have.

## Another Trip Into Kota

Margaret and Bill have a first in the Township! On Saturday, October 10th, they left the kids with a neighbour and went into Kota by motorcycle. (Two people on one motorcycle of course!) The round trip is well over 100 Kilometres (around 65-70 miles?) so it was quite an accomplishment. Besides buying some things Margaret got a fine sunburn on her face, neck and lower lip and both Bill and Margaret were stiff at the other end for several hours on their return. But we saw some interesting things:

(a) Animals:

As well as threading ourselves through the usual herds of cattle, water buffalo, goats and sheep, we stopped within several feet of monkeys, saw a lizard about 2 feet long (including his tail) and ran over a snake. We almost hit half a dozen vultures as they slowly took off the road in front of us as well as several other kinds of birds. You really do see everything on a motorcycle.

(b) Dusshera Fair:

Dusshera is a big Indian holiday in which they celebrate Rama's triumph over the forces of evil. As well as having a country fair resembling the same thing in Canada, they build huge (10 - 20 ft. high) effigies representing the force of evil which was defeated by Rama (according to Indian legend). At dusk these are set on fire and since they are filled with fireworks, they blow up in all directions creating quite a spectacle. Every town and city has their own huge statue to burn in effigy. Rawat Bhata had quite a nice one, but Kota had a huge set of figurines all over 15 ft. high - brightly painted and standing on a wooden stage surrounded by tiered seats. Margaret and Bill stopped on the way out of Kota on Saturday and spent about half an hour walking through the fair. It was absolutely jammed with people - but we were the only non-Indians. We bought several little souvenirs for the children - windmills and toy drums and plastic necklaces and wandered around. There were some amusement rides - a bamboo ferris wheel about ten feet in height that was run by hand - three fellows push it around. There was a simple kind of merry-go-round much like children's playground equipment in Canada with wire seats on it which was pushed by several boys plus one fairly decent Ferris wheel which we saw from a distance. It looks like it might even be run by a motor! There were dozens and dozens of little stalls selling endless varieties of Indian sweets and delicacies, souvenirs, clothing - one place looked just like a rummage sale, jewellery, tools, almost anything you can think of.

Margaret wore slacks because of going on the motorcycle. She was stared at by literally thousands of people during the half hour. After a while though, you get used to being a centre of attraction. It happens every time we go in to Kota. For example, Bill bought a pair of sunglasses from a stand at the side of the road. By the time they were paid for, there were at least twelve people standing around watching. When we got back to the motorcycle we had to pack the saddle bags with our purchases, unlock it, get it started, etc. By the time that was done, we had another dozen in an audience around us - mostly young boys.

Often the Indians that pass you on the street will say whatever English words they know just to impress you. As we went to Kota we had "Hello", "Good Morning", "one, two, three, four", "thank you" and "I love you" all yelled at us in laughter. While we were at the fair, two old men carried on a short but earnest conversation in English saying things such as "Thank you, thank you, good afternoon, yes" etc., purely for our benefit as we passed. Indian people are very friendly and eager to show any knowledge they have of English. If you are friendly back and smile, a trip through any crowded area can be a very interesting experience. You seldom sense any hostility in the people. They are happy, friendly people who like to talk with strangers.

One sad note to our visit. We forgot to take a camera! However, you can be sure we will be to the Dusshera Fair next year with children and camera!

## Latest News on the Car:

Latest letters from the shipping company suggest that our car will likely be replaced with a brand new one which will be shipped as soon as possible. At the moment, the insurance company is causing some delay getting all the official papers and documents completed. Some minor complications may arise with the spare parts order but it does look like we will get a replacement vehicle. No delivery date has been set yet. We are hopeful it will be by Christmas. In the mean time, the motorcycle zooms on!

## A Week of Privation:

Last Thursday night, Bill drove our cook, Mary, into the Kota railway station to go to her brother's wedding (Not on the motorcycle - in a Land Rover borrowed for the evening!) So, for the next few days we must manage with only a sweeper and a gardener! Margaret will actually have to do the cooking! Will Margaret remember how to cook?

Will the Tranter's be able to adjust to this drastic change in their diet - namely Margaret's cooking? Will they survive to write another newsletter? No one knows. Keep watching the mail!

## RAPP Social Life:

Margaret and Bill have been to parties the last two Saturdays in a row. Two weeks ago, the party was held by one of the families in the township. It was an evening of snacks, drinks, dancing, talking and some party games. It culminated at 2:00 a.m. with a dip in the pool! Lots of fun. It was rather chilly really. Evening temperatures get down to around 80.

This Saturday's party was held at the newly completed guest house and was an opportunity for RAPP Township residents to meet with some of the members of the Canadian embassy in Delhi. It was a more formal affair. The evening was a pleasant mixture of food, drinks and conversation.

Other recent activities include several play rehearsals for Bill - some members of the community are planning to present a play in the beginning of December. More about that in a later newsletter.

## Food Supply In Township

During the past few weeks the supplies of meat and other commodities such as butter, ice cream and other frozen foods have been very low. These are usually shipped from Bombay by train, but train schedules have been way off so the store sometimes has practically no meat. Fortunately with our freezer, we have had enough of a backlog of meat to last us over the short supply periods but even our freezer supplies were getting pretty low. Last week an Indian came around offering to sell freshly killed pork. The man was sent to RAPP on the recommendation of the American Peace Corps boys in Kota. The only stipulation was that you had to go into Kota and pick it up on Saturday. So we ordered 2 kilos of chops and 2 kilos of ribs. When we arrived at the Peace Corps house on Saturday the man was sitting on the kitchen floor surrounded in cut up pork ready to cut your order to specifications. He chopped it with an old beat-up axe that was so dull we've seen sharper hammers. Then he cut it with his carving knife. By the way, Indian butchers hold their carving knife between their big toe and first toe and saw the meat back and forth over the blade holding it in both hands. It's quite a feat with your feet! We'll get some pictures of it some time in case you want to try it.

## Closing:

Well we're running out of air mail paper tonight, so we'll close after three pages instead of the usual five. Keep those letters coming. We always like to hear news from that country we used to live in - what was it called? Konada, or something like that. We are all well - at least so far - Marg hasn't cooked any meals for us yet. We look forward to your letters plus any other forms of communication

such as tape recordings, films, pictures, newspaper articles or
whatever. We are going to start work on a tape tomorrow night. We
hope it gets through as well as the films did.

Write soon. Love from,
Margaret, Bill, Jeff, Linda and David.

Our regrets for the long delay between this newsletter and the last. The last two weeks have been very busy around here in business and social life. There never seemed to be an evening free to write a decent letter. So here goes...

## Diwali

A belated Happy Diwali to all of you! In case you don't know, Diwali (the festival of lights) is one of the biggest Indian holidays of the year. It commemorates the Indian God Rama's return to his kingdom after defeating the powers of darkness and ignorance. The people celebrate by cleaning their houses, wearing new clothes, serving special food and lighting candles and letting off fireworks at night. Diwali was celebrated on October 29th but for many Hindus the celebration continued over several days. It is the equivalent, in our custom, to Christmas.

One of the first signs of Diwali was the opening of a number of fireworks displays in Rawat Bhata. Indian fireworks are very good with much more variety than Canadian ones. They still sell sky-rockets of all shapes and sizes (remember those things?). They sell flares, sparklers, all sizes of cannon crackers – some with explosions so loud and bright I wouldn't dare to buy them – and many other unusual ones – like "helicopters" which you light on the ground and they spin around and take off. Another unusual one we had was a "phone express" which you put on a long string between two trees. When you light it, it shoots down the string like a miniature monorail, then stops and comes back. Although the variety is great, they are certainly more dangerous than Canadian fireworks and we had to really supervise when we let them off. We bought quite a good selection (more than we would buy in Canada) for 15 rupees ($2.00).

On the night of Diwali we were invited to bring the children over to the apartment of Mr. and Mrs. K-- (Mrs. K-- is our Indian librarian). We arrived about 7:30 p.m. We were served cold pop and then a variety of at least a dozen kinds of food – some vegetable-like egg rolls and some fried "sweets" a little like cake donuts, etc. They were very tasty and interesting. It wasn't until later in the evening that we realized that the K--s are vegetarians like many Indians and so was all the food we ate! After Diwali snacks Mr. K-- took us out on the balcony of his apartment and let off fireworks so the kids really saw lots of them this year.

## Hallowe'en

Two days after Diwali came the Canadian's celebration of Hallowe'en – and did they ever celebrate it! You have never seen a group of children in such excellent costumes in your life. Probably half were made by the tailor in Rawat Bhata and the other half gave the mothers a lot of work. On Friday, October 30th, the primary classes had a Hallowe'en party in school during the afternoon in which all pre-school children were invited. Of course the mothers came along and it was quite a big event with games, costume judging and refreshments. Linda went as a court jester, Jeff was a king and David was a devil. Costumes for our kids was an easy task - a number of Canadians left costumes at the school when they went back to Canada and our kids chose three of those.

On Saturday night, the children went trick-or-treating. They got a huge bag of candy and junk. Almost every kid in the community went to every Canadian house in the community. We estimated that we had 68 kids at the door.

At 8:15 on the same night, Bill had a Hallowe'en party for his class. It included a "spook house" entrance, games, music, refreshments, etc. It ended around 10:15 p.m. The kids enjoyed themselves, but they were really tired by that time - particularly the grade 5's like Jeff.

Sunday night was the big costume ball for the adults. We thought the kids were all dressed up, but you should have seen the adults! Again, a good many of the costumes were made by the tailor in Rawat Bhata from sketches, pictures, etc. Margaret went as a witch in a big black flowing cape and a black hat. Bill went as a baby in a night gown, diaper, soother, bottle, bonnet, etc. It received a number of interesting comments to say the least. The party was held in the newly completed guest house and music was provided by a full professional dance band imported from Delhi and they were really good. There was lots to eat and drink. Each family brought something to drink and most brought a plate of sandwiches or other suitable snacks. We left early around midnight. The final people left around 4:00 a.m. We are told that attendance was rather poor at plant site on Monday morning!

## Swimming Gala

On Sunday, Nov. 1st, the Canadians held their first swimming gala at the pool in two years. It was a water show including funny skits, demonstrations of swimming strokes, life-saving techniques, diving exhibition and a water ballet by eight of the Canadian ladies. The attendance was excellent. It provided an interesting afternoon of information and entertainment. You remember swimming don't you? That's what you used to do last summer. We're still doing it although the pool is getting a little cold now.

## Motorcycle News

Bill now has over 1,200 Kilometres on his motorcycle. It's running very well. Today he took it on a 50 kilometre cross-country tour that would have been entirely out of the question with any other vehicle. He followed back roads half way around the reservoir with a single set of jeep tracks as proof that the road ahead was usable. On the trip he forded two rivers and climbed several rock-paved hills that would have been impossible for a car. In return for all this trouble, dust, dirt and risks he saw a number of herds of camels, wild monkeys, the usual sheep, water buffalo, cattle, etc., some very old Indian villages and a magnificent view of the reservoir from the edge of a cliff that went straight down for about 200 feet.

Motorcycles are not a novelty around here any more. A number of the recently arrived Hydro workers (Ontario Hydro) brought motor cycles with them. There are three Canadians with Rajdoot Rangers and a variety of imported cycles owned by about 6 Canadians. We'll have to work on some cross-country motorcycle hikes for the men!

Linda's Birthday Party

Linda had a birthday party on October 24th. She invited about 13 girls. They had a typical Canadian birthday party with games, presents and refreshments. Linda got some very nice presents including: two dolls, about 45 bangles, a carved wooden jewellery box, a flashlight, a brooch and necklace and over 40 rupees in cash. Thank you for the birthday cards from Canada too.

Car News

Volkswagen has definitely confirmed that our van will be replaced with a new one at no cost to us. It should be shipped soon. With luck we might have it by Christmas. That was good news. We were getting a little worried about the possibilities of extra shipping charges, demurrage charges on the vehicle here and other costs which might not be covered by insurance but we have been reassured.

## Remember Us?

In response to several requests for a letter to see if we are still alive this newsletter is being written. It is really only 10 days since we sent the last one, but it seems that whenever we are a few days late in writing, the mail service decides to compound our sins by being particularly slow. Let us assure you now:

1. We are all reasonably well. (We have had bad colds but are recovering.)
2. The following reasons are suggested for sending fewer letters recently:
   (a) We are running out of interesting news.
   (b) Things have been really busy around here - both socially and school activities - the second report cards went out yesterday.
   (c) Since everyone had bad colds we didn't feel like staying up to all hours writing letters. (By the way, there is a pile of 8 individual business letters in front of me that I have already written tonight before beginning this one!)
3. The fact that you are not getting regular letters is NOT and never will be a sign that something serious is wrong. You may be sure, that if something is wrong, you will hear about it.

Anyway, I don't feel too badly about not writing every week recently. I was talking to someone tonight who has been in township for three months and still hasn't got around to writing a letter home!

## The Weather

Just a short gloating period before we go on. We were swimming in the outdoor pool for several hours on Sunday. It was very nice. How is the weather in Canada? Ha! Ha! Actually it is beginning to get cooler here. Most evenings the temperature is down in the low sixties. People who have been here for a while complain about the cold! The days, of course, are always sunny and warm. It is really funny to get up every day to the same kind of weather. We went away for the weekend last week and when I got up on the Saturday morning I looked up at the sky and thought "It looks like it's going to be a nice weekend." Then I realized what a foolish thought that was. Every weekend is nice for 10 months of the year around here. Actually they say that the continuous sunny weather gets rather boring after a while and you long for at least a hint of unexpected weather in the form of rain-showers occasionally. We are not to that stage yet. We like it.

## Visitors to the School

There have been lots of visitors to the school recently. We had the federal minister in charge of Atomic Energy for the Indian

Government drop in for a quick tour one day. Two A.E.C.L. people have also been in for more extended visits. Both seemed very pleased with the school. They have also received positive reports from members of the community about the school - so it looks as if Bill's job is secure for the two years! It should be! Both teachers in the school are putting in a lot of work and effort into making the school a success.

## Our Trip to Delhi

Last weekend, November 13, 14, 15, our family went to New Delhi. We left on Thursday night on a little private airline that flies a DC-3 between Kota and Delhi. Marg, Bill and the 3 kids arrived in Delhi around 8:00 p.m. after a two-hour flight.

Delhi is different from every other Indian city. It is the only one that remotely resembles a modern western city. The streets are smoothly paved, wide enough for several lanes of traffic and free from the dirt you expect to see in most Indian cities. The buildings are modern compared to the rest of India and hygienic conditions are such that you can go into any of a large number of restaurants and get good food.

We spent a good bit of our time shopping. The children were pleased to find that Delhi has a wide variety of toy stores with a reasonable selection of toys although none of the elaborate ones they advertise on Canadian and American t.v. We bought a small bicycle for David and a variety of other things including rubber tires for the motorcycle (out of stock in Kota), motorcycle crash helmets for Bill and one children's size, goggles, dress material, souvenirs, two enamelled brass lamps, several Christmas gifts, etc., etc.

On Friday night we went to the circus playing in Delhi. It was quite a good one with trapeze artists, trained animal acts, motorcycle stunt drivers, clowns and so on. We sat in the very best reserved seats for Rs. 5.50 each (about 75¢). The kids thought it was great. Indian circuses are even bigger on snacks than Canadian ones. You could buy popcorn, potato chips, nuts, cokes, orange drink, tea, cakes, Indian delicacies, chocolate bars, candy, etc. etc. The kids had a great time and ate like pigs. The circus lasted almost three hours. It was a real experience.

## The Delhi Zoo

The Delhi Zoo was our choice for sight-seeing on Sunday afternoon. It is a huge rambling zoo of over 250 acres in the city built on the ruins of an old fort. In fact some of the walls of the animal compounds are remnants of the old fort walls. The only problem is, that because of the size of the zoo, it is difficult to get around to see very much without walking for miles. We saw the best parts though - the white Indian tigers (Albino) that are so famous. There were at least half a dozen there. We saw elephants, lions, monkeys, many varieties of birds, etc. The kids got their picture taken holding on to the tusk of a huge elephant. Apparently they have elephant rides for the children, but they were not operating while we were there.

## Sound and Light Show at the Red Fort

Sunday night we went to the Red Fort to see a combination of coloured flood lights and tape recorded narrative and sound effects outlining the history of the Red Fort in the past two hundred years.

The Red Fort is a truly impressive sight. It is a huge series of buildings surrounded by a reddish sandstone wall that has been the seat of Indian government for over two hundred years. We hope to go back and see more of it again.

Delhi was a very pleasant change from the rest of India. We enjoyed the feeling of being back in real civilization. That would be the perfect way to come to India if you decide to come and visit us. From Delhi is is only two hours by plane to township.

## Food

Hotels in Delhi really cater to the tourists. As a result we ordered steak, filet mignon and other similarly exotic items (by Indian standards) which are unavailable in other parts of India. For example, it is against the law to slaughter beef for food in Rajasthan. You can go to jail for 20 years for killing a cow with your car. There is a 5-year jail term for killing a peacock - the national bird - and there are lots of those wandering about on the roads too.

## A Warning:

If you have friends that wish to see India, be sure they do not simply plan a one-stop trip to Delhi to find out about India. Delhi is nice, but it is not what India is really like. It is a showpiece for the rest of the world - not the real country at all. It is in the smaller cities - such as Kota - and in the countryside that you see what India and Indians are really like.

## Pictures:

We've been taking lots of picture recently - mainly coloured slides which are in Bombay for processing. If possible, we'll organize a slide plus tape presentation to send home by Christmas. More information about that in the future.

## Latest News on the Car:

We got a letter today saying that our Volkswagen Van will be shipped from Germany on December 3rd and should arrive in Bombay around the 20th of January. So it looks like we'll definitely get our new car, but not for two months at least.

In the mean time, the motorcycle is still running very well.

## A Brave Family:

On Monday, John Stevens - an A.E.C.L. supervisor - and his family arrived at site. They left England in late September with three children in a Fargo camper and drove all the way! You can imagine some of the experiences they must have had. He gave us a little half-hour talk on it the other night and it sounds like a tremendous experience for anyone hardy enough to attempt it. They had a few exciting incidents like their car being stoned in one of the Arab countries but there were no serious problems. The camper ran very well - no flat tires and only one minor mechanical problem.

They will be living in Bombay but John will be up to site regularly to supervise the work here.

## Christmas:

It's hard to believe Christmas is only a month away. There are none of the signs around here such as the store decorations, coloured lights, Santa Claus parade, etc. and of course, with no television, you don't get continual reminders here either. We plan to spend Christmas at site. We have our artificial tree and we plan to celebrate much as we would at home. We may visit Jaipur or Jodhpur between Christmas and New Year's. We will use the old DC-3 again.

## Question Corner:
Here are some of the prize-winning questions from the past two weeks:

Q: How did things go at the Hallowe'en Party? (C. J--)
A: We had a great time. Bill was adorable in his baby costume. Comments varied on it from adorable to obscene. Marg was a witch - black hat, cloak, and long black straggly hair. At the kid's party David was a devil, Linda a court jester and Jeffrey a king.

Q: When you go for a ride on the motorcycle, how about the little ones left behind? (C. J--)

A: Motorcycle rides are on a strict rotational basis for the children. There are very few long trips. By the way, Margaret had her first lesson on it a week ago. She can drive it in low gear! Wow!

Q: How did the cooking go when Mary was in Bombay? (C. J--)
A: (From Bill) It was ~~terrible~~ great! Margaret always was a ~~terrible~~ great cook and she's still just as ~~bad~~ good. By the way, Margaret has hired a dhobi[18] to do her ironing two half-days a week because it was too much for her. Can you imagine that? I told her that when I go back to Canada I'll bring the cook, sweeper, dhobi and mali[19] and leave Marg behind.

Q: Will you bring your motorcycle back to Canada? (C T--)
A: No. Motorcycles are great for Indian weather. They're not worth it in Canada. Also there would be real complications for parts and servicing.

Q: Did you feel any of the effects of the Pakistan typhoon?
A: No, it was much too far away, but the papers were full of it. It was really a disaster.

Q: What happened to D-- and D--'s tape recording? (Bill)
A: We don't know. Can you answer that one?

Well that's about all for now. Write soon. Love,

> Margaret, Bill
> Jeff, Linda, David.

P.S. Today was a big day in Township. Imported "Smarties" in the store. All the kids were eating them. Only Rs. 1.35 per pack! That's 20¢ for about the 5¢ size.

---

18  A washerman or washerwoman.
19  Gardener.

As head teacher at the Rajasthan township school Bill Tranter finds that supervising 48 Canadian children is a big job. Here he takes time out from work to ride an elephant with his wife Margaret and two of his three children, Linda and David.

# A hotter class

**BY STEVE LYNETT**
**Staff writer**

Etobicoke teacher Bill Tranter thinks he has a unique school situation.

It isn't just that the temperature in his classroom reaches 100 degrees or that he's teaching his own children. It's more than that.

His school is in India.

And it's there because 48 Canadian children need the munity built specially for the project, they set up in a new home and began to adjust to a totally new life style.

From letters sent to friends and relatives in Canada it appears the community is a happy one as well as a well organized one.

The school is not only the centre of eucational life in the community but it is also a prime gathering area for word in a school such as Tranter's, the problems encountered also fall into that category.

Supplies remain one of the major headaches of the operation.

In a recent report to Etobicoke Board of Education Tranter said that if the school is to maintain the standards of an Ontario curriculum increased help and guidance of a Canadian teacher.

The children are sons and daughters of Ontario Hydro and Atomic Energy of Canada employees helping to commission a 400,000 kilowatt nuclear station at Rajasthan.

Tranter is on loan from the Etobicoke board of Education and is legally an Etobicoke employee but for all intents and purposes he's on his own.

His school consists of two classrooms a small library and a study room as well as three other gathering rooms. The operation is by no means well off but the curriculum which Tranter, as head teacher, has designed will allow the children an easy re-entry into the Ontario system.

Formerly vice principal at Briarcrest public school in Etobicoke, Tranter not only runs the school but he teaches 22 of its students in grades 5 to 8.

Mrs. Elaine White, the other Canadian teacher, is responsible for 26 students in grades 1 to 4.

And their work is supplemented by an Indian librarian and teacher's aide, Mrs. Rani Kapurand and an Indian caretaker, Shri Gokul.

Tranter and the power-plant crew arrived in Rajasthan in the summer of 1970. Like the project engineers, Tranter took with him his wife Margaret and three children Linda, David and Jeff.

There, in a closed com-social activities.

For the children the classrooms closely resemble those found in most small Canadian centres. The school day is basically the same as that in Canada with the exception of the temperature which turns recess into a rest period.

According to Tranter, the recess bell doesn't spark a mad rush for the door but a rather slow exodus from the classroom into adjoining areas of the school.

The children settle for "chess, blackboard games, talking or just sitting around" rather than go outside where it is often 10 to 15 degrees hotter.

Tranter describes his stay at the school as the "most interesting and challenging period" in his life and said that on arriving he discovered the situation far better than had been described to him.

Tranter said Etobicoke's emphasis on the integrated learning program in the past few years has provided him with an effective approach to the multi-graded classroom.

He not only deals well with the students but because of the small community he is constantly in touch with the parents.

With only 30 families in the community, discussions on such matters as pupil progress not only become very informal but they become more frequent.

People are surprised to find that a teacher is just like everyone else.

Since unique is the key supplies will have to be imported.

Although sources of school supplies do exist in India, they are only found in the large centres such as Bombay and New Delhi. For this reason Tranter must travel to the cities several times a year to order and arrange for their delivery.

And what he cannot get in India he must get from Canada. Textbooks, workbooks, records, courses of study and audio visual aids all must be imported.

For Tranter, the matter of predicting the kinds and amounts of equipment and supplies needed, presents a serious problem. There is a time lapse which makes long term planning extremely difficult.

An order placed to Canada usually takes about six months to arrive after it is assembled shipped, cleared through customs and delivered to the site.

Ordering of equipment such as desks, book shelves and bulletin boards is equally time consuming since staff must include detailed drawings of them. That's so the items can be manufactured to meet the school's specifications.

And he noted that in the case of student desks one order took seven months for delivery.

Because it is the only one of its kind in India, the school's children are unable to interact with a wide variety of children possessing their own cultural background.

*Figure 2: A newspaper article about our family's trip that appeared in an Etobicoke community newspaper some time in 1971.*

# MERRY CHRISTMAS AND HAPPY NEW YEAR! [20]

Christmas Greetings from Rajasthan, India. By the time you get this letter we will have been in India for five months. We are having a most enjoyable time but, of course, we will miss the family get-togethers at this time of year.

Christmas weather is rather different here than in Canada. There is not a hint of snow! Day time temperatures are in the seventies and eighties. At night it gets down into the fifties or sixties. Every day is sunny and warm. There has been no rain for four months and none is expected for five months more. However, this poses no problem for us since we live within sight of a water reservoir over twenty miles long.

India has little to remind us of a Canadian Christmas and yet we are rather pleased at the thought of spending the season in weather conditions much like those in Bethlehem at the time of the birth of Jesus. It adds a new realism to the Christmas story when it is told in this climate.

In case you are wondering how we will spend Christmas Day, here are our plans. We will have Christmas decorations, lights and our artificial tree (purchased last April for inclusion in our sea shipment). The children will get presents from Santa Claus as usual - some imported from Canada when we came and saved for the occasion and some purchased in India. We will have our Christmas dinner with turkey and all of the trimmings at about 1:30 with a number of families in the community gathering at the large guest house to celebrate together. We will probably spend the afternoon singing Christmas carols, playing party games, etc. much like home. One big difference will be that Christmas dinner will be cooked, served and cleaned up by the staff of the guest house although some of the ladies will undoubtedly want to contribute their favourite Christmas recipes to the menu. Because of the weather, we can consider some outdoor games such as croquet for the children during the afternoon. But you can be sure that this is one day when everyone in the community will miss the sight of crisp white snow spread over the countryside.

We have had quite an active time since we arrived in India. We returned to Bombay for almost a week of shopping and sight-seeing in early October. In late November the whole family went to New Delhi for sight-seeing and shopping again. Of course there have been many short trips to local places of interest as well as almost weekly visits to the nearest Indian city, Kota. Many more trips are planned to cities such as Jaipur, Jodhpur, Agra and Bundi. We hope to visit Kashmir during the summer holidays. For many of these trips we hope to use our new Volkswagen Camping Van. In case you haven't heard, our new van, ordered through Germany, was severely damaged on the ship

---

20  This Christmas letter was printed on a spirit duplicator ("Ditto") machine and sent to a larger group of people than the others that only went to our immediate relatives and therefore repeats some information that was in previous letters.

before it reached Bombay. Damage was so extensive that the car is to be replaced with a new 1971 model. In the mean time, our family travels short distances two at a time on our Indian motorcycle, the Rajdoot Ranger. Bill can drive it and Margaret is learning.

The children, Jeff, Linda and David, seem to be really enjoying their stay in India. Everyone agrees that the community is ideal for children with its well-equipped school, playground, swimming pool, recreation hall, etc. They have lots of friends and are all well-tanned and healthy-looking. They are looking forward to Christmas, but there is not the big build-up to the Christmas season here that there is in Canada since there is no television, large department stores, decorated streets, etc. Here, the Christmas spirit kind of sneaks up on you just a week or so before the big day. It is the same delayed Christmas spirit that left us sending our Christmas cards so late.

We will be thinking of you on Christmas day. Best wishes for the holiday season and good luck in the year 1971. From,

Margaret, Bill, Jeff, Linda & David Tranter

HAPPY NEW YEAR!

Here we are starting out the new year right with a newsletter on the first day. How about that! It's 9:30 p.m. The children are nestled all snug in their beds. It has been a typical day of hardship in India. Temperature in the high 70's. A turkey dinner this evening with cranberry sauce (imported), baked potatoes, creamed cauliflower, fresh cabbage salad and so on with lemon pie for dessert. Now I'm sitting here sipping cherry brandy (not imported) and writing a newsletter on behalf of the family. We hope you had a happy new year. There will be more about ours below. This letter is designed to tell you about our first Christmas in India.

CHRISTMAS EVE

Christmas Eve was very much like at home. We stayed home until 7:00 p.m. when we went down to the outdoor badminton court for the regular Thursday night township English movie (English-speaking that is - American produced usually). We saw a slightly antiquated movie called Countdown about an astronaut going to the moon. It wasn't great but the kids liked it because it was in technicolor with lots of spacecraft, etc. We came home at nine and the children went to bed. Marg and I wrapped Christmas gifts, did other Christmas Eve-type things. Marg did some final baking. I worked on the Christmas party games I was organizing. At 11:30 p.m., dressed in my good green suit I went to Christmas midnight mass at the recreation hall. I was invited to attend to lead the carol singing but I would have probably gone anyway. It was a nice service - not really very different from the Anglican Christmas Eve service except for the sermon. If you think sermons can be trying in Canada you should try India. We listened to a fairly short but uninspired sermon and then we had to listen to it all over again in Hindi!

I came home at around 12:30. We finished wrapping gifts and went to bed around 1:30 a.m.

CHRISTMAS MORNING:

Christmas morning the kids were up at 7:30 to see what Santa Claus had brought. Fortunately Santa had planned well ahead last April so the children got such things as: a Johnny Astro (Bill's favourite toy), Mattel picture-maker kits, twin twirler tops, Barbie doll, a good variety of Canadian toys. Linda got a set of Indian woven baskets that fit inside each other. The boys got turbans. They got a carom game between the three of them. Carom, in case you don't know, is an Indian game played on a board something like crokinole but with four corner pockets. The object of the game is to hit the round markers into the corner pockets. It is very much like a combination of pool and crokinole. Very challenging. We'll teach you how to play when we come home.

Of course we all opened some gifts given to us before we left Canada. Margaret and I didn't plan to exchange gifts. Instead we decided to save our money for a trip to Jaipur. Margaret bought me a nice cardigan sweater, however, making me feel rotten for not buying her anything. The morning was spent happily with Bill trying to get the kids to let him play with their toys as usual.

At 1:30 we went up to the guest house and joined about 75 other Canadians for a Christmas dinner of turkey, etc. in the guest house dining room. This was followed by a carol sing and group games organized and led by Bill (just like at home but for 75 people instead of abut 15!) The dinner and games were a great success and everyone really had a much better time than they expected to have on Christmas so far from home. The children particularly enjoyed the dinner and games although everyone participated.

The party ended at about 5:45 p.m. We came home. The children played with their toys again and we got the place cleaned up. After the kids were in bed we had 7 friends in for a fondue supper. It lasted from 9:00 until 12:00 and was enjoyed by all. We cooked tenderloin (of water buffalo) in fondue dishes and had salads, bread, Christmas baking and so on. A highlight of the evening was everyone's turn on the Johnny Astro space station.

So ended a very full Christmas day in India, made somewhat easier by help from our cook and our sweeper.

By the way we gave our Mali a sweater, our cook a portable transistor radio and our sweeper a cardigan sweater for Christmas.

Our Trip to Jaipur

Saturday and Sunday were spent recovering from Christmas and preparing for our trip to Jaipur, the "Pink City". We left Monday afternoon in a D.A.E. (Dept. Of Atomic Energy) station wagon for the Kota Airport at about 4:00 p.m. After a somewhat hazardous ride – the vehicle, like all D.A.E. vehicles at site, was falling apart – we arrived at the airport and took a local plane to Jaipur – a 50-minute trip. There was a little extra excitement in taking this plane because just a week and a half before the other plane making the same run crashed killing 5 people including the pilot and co-pilot. In spite of that we figured it was safer than our wild ride from Township in the D.A.E. station wagon!

We arrived in Jaipur around 7:30 p.m. and proceeded to the Rambagh Palace – a real palace which has been converted to a hotel.

It was very nice and we were fortunate to get rooms since we didn't have a reservation. We went out to dinner at Niro's, a very nice Americanized restaurant in the city and then we went to bed. The following morning we shopped – we didn't buy much but some nice brassware, ivory and jewellery. In the afternoon we hired a private car and guide (very exclusive!) and took a tour of the city which included the city palace including the observatory and 3 museums and other sights of interest like the Palace of Winds (check your National Geographic for pictures of that).

The next morning we went about 5 miles outside of Jaipur to the Amber Fort and travelled up to the Fort by elephant. Our private guide gave us a thorough tour of the Fort and we returned to our private car by private elephant (see picture!).

In the afternoon we went shopping again. We bought an Opal ring for Linda (her birthstone), an aquamarine ring for Margaret, an enamelled brass tray and two brass footstools and several other items. By this time we had moved to another converted palace called the Jai Mahal Palace because the Rambagh was full. It was not quite as elaborate as the Rambagh but the service and food were excellent. We left the hotel at 6:45 a.m. on Wednesday morning to catch the plane back to Kota and arrived home after another trip in a D.A.E. vehicle (this time very slow and cautious) at around 10:30 a.m.

New Year's Eve

On New Year's Eve two families went together and invited all Canadians in Township to a New Year's Eve barbecue. They made elaborate preparations having about 10 barbecues made and buying almost 100 metres of turban material to make a tent-like covering over their patio. There was dancing and socializing with about 25 couples from 9:30 p.m. until about 5:00 a.m. for some. Most left around 2:00 a.m. as we did. It was a great party and we hauled in the New Year while you people were still finishing lunch at 1:30 in the afternoon on New Year's Eve.

New Year's Day

Today was a very quiet day in township. Many people slept for most of the day. We recovered quite well. The only outstanding event was our New Year's Dinner at home as I described above.

The one thing I didn't mention was the cost of the turkey. The turkey weighed just under 8 pounds (including head and feet) and cost over 100 rupees (about $15.00). As you can imagine, we don't have turkey very often!

## A Formal Dance

This coming Sunday evening, township residents are finishing up the holiday celebrations with a formal dance at the guest house. We are bringing the band down from New Delhi. All the ladies will wear formal dresses (if Marg gets hers made in time). The men will wear suits. We won't recognize each other. It is so unusual to see a suit jacket or tie around here that it should be a real occasion. One man even attended the Christmas dinner in shorts and a sports shirt.

## Car News

We now have our car keys and license plates. The ship is due on the 19th of January. Assuming the usual amount of time for unloading, customs, clearance, etc. we should have our car by mid-February.

## A Word About Cheques and Money Orders

Although we appreciate receiving gifts such as cheques and money orders, we think you should know that they are really quite difficult to cash. Even when drawn in rupees, cheques must be presented to the bank in Rawat Bhata. There we have to fill in all sorts of forms. Then the cheques are sent to Bombay for processing and hopefully the money will eventually be added to our Rawat Bhata bank account. So far we haven't been able to cash any of the cheques although all of them are in the process of being sent to Bombay for clearance, etc. Although we appreciate the thought, when we consider the effort at that end as well, it probably isn't worth the time involved to send us cheques while we're in India.

## How About Your Christmas?

We're looking forward to hearing about your Christmas. If you haven't written yet with news about the holiday season in Canada, get at it now. We'd like to hear about it.

Goodbye for now.
Love,
Marg, Bill, Jeff, Linda, David

Dear G--, P--, S-- & G--

    I am enclosing a pair of earrings that we bought for G-- in Jaipur. They are enamelled metal which is one of the handicrafts that Jaipur is well known for. They were very inexpensive so if by some chance they are removed from this letter it is nothing to worry about.

    Well I have finally given up and started playing bridge. Of the 12 women on the street only 3 of us didn't play and since it is the main pastime here, I found that we were really left out. So I finally gave in to all the urging and have started to play. The only trouble is that you could spend every afternoon playing bridge and I don't intend to do that.

              Love Bill & Marg

It Was a Tough Winter!

Hello to all our dear relatives in Canada! You will be pleased to know that our Indian friends tell us that Winter ends on the 15th of January. From now on the weather gets warmer quite quickly. It's a real relief to have it over with you can be sure. Why, some days it only went up to the high 70's - and evenings got so cold that we needed a blanket on our bed if the window was open! Brrr! However, that's all past now. Spring is here. The last few days have already shown signs of warmer weather. Is winter over in Canada yet? If not, I guess the grass will be getting green pretty soon.

In this country the countryside is very brown and dusty at this time of year. There has been no rain for 5 months. The earth is dry and rocky. It is difficult to believe that the same rocky, barren fields we cross on the way to school were so thick with grass we had to keep to the path when we arrived. The only splashes of green are the lawns in township and farmers' fields that have methods of irrigation - usually a water buffalo pulling a leather bag of water from a water tank or well.

Things will get much dryer before we see rain. In May, we hope to take some colour slides of some typical scenes in the community, then go back to the same spots right after monsoon so that you can see the dramatic changes.

Every day sunny and warm is really grand. It is going to be really difficult to get used to Canada again where you can never be sure if a picnic or camping trip will be cancelled because of rain. Here it is a real occasion to see a cloud in the sky. Most days the sky is completely blue. In the distance there is a permanent haze all the time but no clouds. The haze may very well be dust rather than moisture in the sky.

It took a while to get used to the very dry air even this close to a reservoir but we're used to it now.


So You Won't Feel So Bad

Occasionally we feel we should tell you some of the disadvantages of living in R.A.P.P. Township so you will realize that the rosy picture we paint in these letters isn't entirely true. In fact, if we play up our problems enough, you may start feeling sorry for us! So read the points below and realize what a hard time we really have. Sob! Sob!

1.  Our food bill this month was one thousand and eight hundred and fifty rupees (over $260.00) not including milk, part of our meat and some extras we buy in Rawat Bhata. Since our monthly allowance in India is $300.00 it is difficult to make ends meet on our Indian salary - sob! If you wonder why it is so high, take the cost of imported cheese for example. A 3-lb. block of

Dutch Gouda cheese was selling in the store today for $8.50. We didn't buy it, of course. We did, however, buy 3 jars of English jam at 9 rupees ($1.25) per jar because most Indian jam is pretty bad.

2. Recent illnesses and operations among Canadians have been at a high level. During the last month, three Canadians have had their appendix out. At least three children have had mild cases of malaria in the last 6 weeks. One lady has a broken toe (from running upstairs and tripping). Two Canadian men are visiting the hospital in Bombay with undiagnosed but reasonably serious illnesses. Nearly everyone has had a cold (from the freezing weather, undoubtedly). Fortunately the Tranter family has so far been afflicted with nothing more serious than minor sprains, colds, etc. We are certainly above average for health in the township.

3. The quality of Indian manufactured goods occasionally leaves something to be desired. Since we purchased bicycles for Jeff and Linda and David, Bill has an almost full-time job keeping them in running condition. Jeff has had three flat tires on his front tire alone! David has had both pedals replaced. Linda's bike, at present sits in the garage with two flat tires. The only consolation is that the cheap spare parts don't cost very much either. Two new pedals for David's bike cost a total of 7 rupees ($1.00).

4. The threat of wild animals is also a constant danger in township. Last Sunday night we heard a terrible roar from down in the valley. It sounded like a tiger had attacked a water buffalo. Of course, being thoroughly frightened, Bill immediately jumped into a neighbour's car and they roared down the trail – it remotely resembles a road – to look for the big cat. However, they had no luck. They saw one camel – with two riders leaving the scene quickly – and one rabbit. Big deal. BUT you can see that we could be attacked by tigers, panthers, or jackals at any time.
   There are jackals in the township every night. One night Bill saw three on the way home from a neighbour's house at 11:00 p.m. They run when they see someone coming but they raid the garbage cans when there's no-one around.

We hope this is enough so you can tell your friends what a hard time your poor relatives are having in India. What a sacrifice! What devotion to duty! We should be missionaries!

News About the Car

There is no news about the car. It was due in Bombay 2 days ago. We hope they haven't dropped it off the ship into the ocean but they probably have with our luck in cars. If not, we may have our car before the next newsletter. We hope so. Do you feel like you've read this before?

## Cubs

David and Jeff are both Wolf Cubs now. There is an active "pack" of boys in township. They meet Saturday mornings. Since the weather is good for outings at this time of year (not too hot) they have been on bicycle hikes for the last two Saturday meetings. Today they rode to Saddle Dam - several miles away - and walked up the ridge of hills to the look-out tower. Then had their lunch and came home at 11:00 a.m. As you can imagine they had a rather early lunch.

Last week they rode their bikes to Rawat Bhata to visit the nearby Baroli Temples. Jeff had a flat on the way and came home by car with his bike. David made it all the way there and back just losing a pedal as he came around the corner home. One of the cub leaders had an odometer on the bicycle. It registered 18 miles when they returned. Quite a trip for a 6½ year old. David had a camel ride while he was in Rawat Bhata.

## Square Dancing

We still go square dancing every Friday night. We are really good now. If you know anybody that needs lessons, just have them see us when we get back to Canada. We know about a dozen really advanced square dances now and we learn several new ones every week. Numbers have dwindled so that our average turn-out is only four or five couples. Part of the problem is we're so good everyone else is afraid to come. Does that sound like conceit - it isn't! Just good honest appreciation of ourselves. Toot! Toot!

## Township Variety Show

Bill has been busy for the past three weeks working on skit scripts for the Township Variety Show in February (13th and 14th). It will be a combination of songs, dances, skits and slapstick humour for the entertainment of all township people plus visitors from Kota. More about that in later letters.

## Christmas Presents

Did you get our Christmas presents? We sent presents to all adults and children on our regular newsletter list. However, some were rather late being mailed so they may not have arrived by Christmas. A few went by sea mail in September. The rest went by air mail in December. You should have them by now. If not, let us know because they were all sent by registered mail.

## Bill's Birthday

Bill sends his thanks to all those that remembered his birthday with greetings from Canada. It was a depressing day because of his extreme old age. May all of you who reminded him that he was thirty-one die a slow and painful death at an early age!

## More About Animals

In case you don't realize how plentiful the animals are around here, we give you this account of a 30-minute motorcycle ride which Bill and David took on Wednesday night just before dinner.

They left township and went down to the valley below our street (where the tiger was heard). On the way down the hill they saw at least 15 monkeys sitting in the trees. As soon as they started along the road in the valley they saw half a dozen peacocks wandering around. Part way down the road they saw 2 jackals or hyenas - we're not sure which - looking at them from 30 yards away through the trees. Then they passed several camels - camels are so common around here now you never take a trip to Rawat Bhata without seeing at least a couple and sometimes huge herds of them. Then as they got close to submersible bridge they flushed about 6 quail or partridge or some type of ground game bird from a thicket beside the road. After fording the stream on the motorcycle (without getting wet, too!) they drove to submersible bridge where they saw a crocodile and a gavial. What's a gavial, you may ask? It is a narrow-snouted, fish-eating relative of the crocodile that grows to an average adult size of 15 feet. Look it up in the encyclopedia. We see them almost every time we go by submersible bridge. There were also more monkeys sitting on the wall chattering as we passed them at submersible bridge. The ride home was quiet with few animals other than the local farm variety of sheep, goats, cattle, water buffalo, etc. Anyway, it's fun to explore the country-side as you can imagine. Remember, we were only gone for a little over half an hour.

## Trudeau Came to India

Trudeau[21] came to India but not to R.A.P.P. Township so we all hate him. Several Canadians went to Delhi to see him there. They spoke to him at the airport. One girl in Bill's class spoke to Mrs. Gandhi (India's Prime Minister) and Mr. Trudeau. When asked what she thought of Trudeau, she replied, "He's ugly!". What happened to all that charm?

Actually there were a number of political reasons for Trudeau wishing to avoid any close contact with Indian Atomic Energy matters. Canada and India are embroiled in discussions about heavy water - the fuel used in the reactors - so he likely didn't want to get going on that topic while he was here. But we were all disappointed anyway. The largest aggregation of Canadians in India and he didn't come and say hello. Boo hoo!

## What About You?

Well, that's about all for now. Anyone driven past our house recently? Is it still there? Have you all recovered from Christmas? Don't forget to send us any local news items that would be of interest. American and national news are pretty well covered in our

---

21  Pierre, not Justin (for the benefit of our younger readers).

daily(?) paper, the Times of India, and with our subscriptions to Time and Newsweek magazines. Local news is a rarity though, so send us anything of interest. Good-bye for now!

Bill & Marg, Jeff, Linda & David

## A Newsy Week

This has been a good week for news from home. We received letters from almost everyone on our regular mailing list plus getting confirmation that most of our Christmas presents arrived (in various conditions) and that the six latest films arrived. We were worried about those because they were our European films as well as two of Christmas in township.

We also received slides and a tape from Briarcrest[22] school giving some information about the fall term and we received the tape V-- made on Christmas night at the T--'s party.

Things have been happening around here too, so we've got lots to write about. One question though... While we were in Jaipur we sent post cards to each of our regular customers. Did you get them? Nobody mentioned them? *[Handwritten note: Yes, several did so I think they got there alright.]*


## Republic Day

January 26th is a big day in India - It commemorates the formation of India as a self-governing republic. In New Delhi there is always a great parade on that day. Many people from township went. We didn't. We stayed home for a four-day weekend. Bill got caught up on some of his school work. We went on a couple of motorcycle hikes and we went to a party and a school concert.

The party was held by the Kota Guards - a soldiers' training centre in Kota. The officers are - or would like to be - quite friendly with the township people. Rumour is that a few years ago one of the officers had an affair with one of the township wives thereby encouraging all officers to make friends with township people and involve them in their social events so they could have affairs too. So far they haven't had any more luck, but the officers certainly go out of their way to make township residents - particularly the women - very welcome at their parties. The party was held partly out-of-doors and partly in the guards quarters. The outdoor part had a band shell, outdoor bar and a dance floor. There were two pipe bands (bagpipes in India? Yes!) and a dance band. Inside there were two more bars and a number of lounges decorated with war relics and hunting trophies - three beautiful tiger heads and several skins. At around 11:30 p.m. there was a tasty cold buffet and it looked like the party would continue for hours more. There were all sorts of dances and elimination contests planned with prizes but we left around 12:30 with our neighbours who had been kind enough to drive us in since we don't have a car yet. Sob! Sob! Anyway it was quite a good party. About 10 Canadian couples were there plus U.N. people, etc. The Kota Guards Officers looked smart in their dress uniforms - particularly Colonel Singh, the commanding officer.

---

22  Bill had been Vice Principal at Briarcrest Public School in Etobicoke, Ontario before going to India.

The strangest thing at the party was to see Indian bagpipe players standing around the outside of the dance floor outdoors while Indian couples did their variations of Scottish dances to Scottish bagpipe tunes. The British influence in India was certainly very strong in the armed forces.

A SCHOOL CONCERT

On the following evening Jeffrey and Bill (Marg wasn't feeling well) attended an annual concert of the R.A.P.P. English Medium School - a school several miles away where the pupils are taught in both Hindi and English but with an emphasis on the English. We received a formal invitation from the principal to attend.

The program included an English play, a Hindi play, songs, Rajasthan folk dances, and for the little children a presentation which they call "Fancy Dress Items" in which 5 - 7 year olds dress up in costumes like we would on Hallowe'en and go up on stage one at a time and say some little thing appropriate to their costume. Some of the lines were in Hindi and some in English. Children varied from just a few words to a whole little skit. The judges then awarded prizes to the best three.

Lots of other prizes were awarded too. The school has about 450 pupils and they must have given out almost 450 silver cups, trophies, certificates and books as prizes for everything you could think of. This was also the occasion of scouting awards. Jeffrey won the award as best cub of the year in the Canadian pack and the presentation was made there.

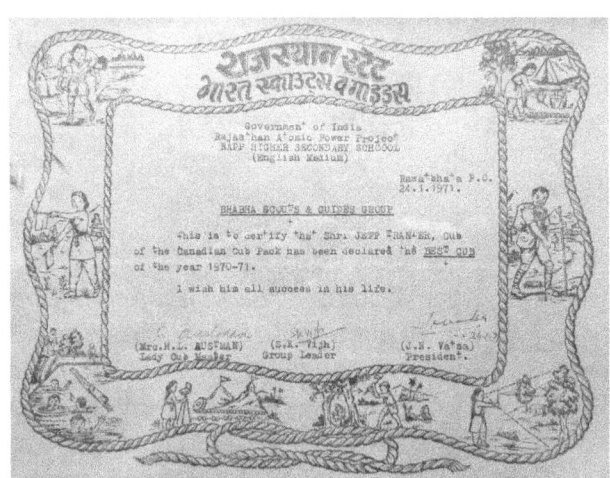

The show started just after 7:00 p.m. and ended at 10:30 p.m. They really went all out. Since they don't have an auditorium they had a big marquee set up plus another smaller one with stage facilities including a raised platform, curtains, lights, and about 5 microphones. It was a very ambitious effort and well worth attending.

A Wild Cat Fight

Do you know what Indian wild cats look like? They are grey with black stripes and just a little larger than a house cat. A week ago we were out visiting for the evening. At around 1:00 a.m. we were just getting ready to leave when we heard this terrible yowling sound outside. Bill, being the brave one, looked out the side door and saw two of these wild cats standing on the road at the end of the driveway. There were either having an argument or were involved in mutual love calls. Anyway, they wouldn't move. We went outside, started the motorcycle, shone lights on them and even threw stones at them and they wouldn't move more than a few feet. They just continued to let out hideous howls at each other. I suggested to our neighbour that he take a picture. He went to get his camera and then remembered that he had loaned his lens to a friend. He suggested that Bill get his camera, so he got on the motorcycle, drove right past them, went up the hill, into the house, got his camera equipment and came back down and they were still there. He got the flash unit all attached, aimed the camera and nothing happened. The flash failed. Just then the cats decided to have a fight and they both shot up the road towards the playground area. So there were no pictures to record it. However, there were lots of witnesses. The people across the street also watched the whole thing from their windows. Apparently it is quite common to see these wild cats in township at night. A number of people have found them on the road or in their garages, etc. They have never attacked anyone but they look quite fierce even if they are small. Anyone want a wild cat skin as a souvenir?

Supply Teaching

Margaret is back in the teaching racket. On Wednesday, E-- W--, the primary teacher was still in Delhi so Margaret took her class for the day. Then E-- was quite sick on Friday so Margaret taught for the day again. She enjoyed it but she doesn't want to do it too often.

After some pushing from Bill, A.E.C.L. agreed to pay for supply teachers, but Bill didn't expect to have to put in the first claim for his own wife. Now he doesn't know whether to bother or not.

NEWS ABOUT OUR CAR!

There is no news about our car.

QUESTION CORNER:

This was a good week for questions in the letters. Here are a few prize-winning ones.

Q: How did you get up on the elephant in Jaipur? (Mrs. C. T--)
A: There is a concrete platform with steps going up. You climb the steps and the elephant comes right over against the edge of the platform. Then you just step in like into a ride at the exhibition. There is a similar loading and unloading area at the end of the trip. So it is really quite simple. In other places where you ride

elephants getting up on it can be quite difficult. Even when they get down on their knees it can be quite a job trying to scramble up on it. There was an elephant around Kota and Rawat Bhata that offered rides. Some people couldn't get up on it at all. It had one good trick though. When you paid at the end of the ride, the elephant took the money from you with its trunk.

Q: How do you get down off an elephant?
A: You don't get down off an elephant, silly, you get down off a duck! (Joke courtesy C. T--, famous old joke teller.)

Q: What are the values of the stamps you send? (Mrs. C. T--)
A: There are two short forms to look for on the stamp that tell you the denominations. "Rs." means rupees. A rupee is worth about 15¢. The "P" means paise. There are a hundred paise in a rupee. In fact Indians use rupees and paise as we use dollars and cents. You pronounce paise (pie-suh) not like that stupid! So, as we were saying, a paise is 1/00 of 15¢.

Q: Do you still have those little lizards in your house? (Mrs. C. T--)
A: Those lizards, called geckos, are regular inhabitants of our house. There are probably at least six that live in our house permanently. Whenever we get one out in the open we usually chase it outside but there are still lots around. One night last week, Bill saw three different ones in the house in less than 10 minutes. They are not very helpful in killing insects and they leave droppings all over the place so we try to discourage them but they come out mainly at night so you don't see them too much. Of course they crawl all over your face and body when you are asleep, sucking your blood whenever possible, but other than that they are not harmful.

Q: How are the insects at this time of year? (Margaret Tranter)
A: There are very few insects around right now. An occasional house fly or mosquito, but hardly any at all. That is also true of snakes, scorpions, etc. The pests seem to come out most during monsoon and just after.

Q: How is the weather there? (Bill Tranter)
A: Weather has been quite chilly this week - well down into the fifties at night. Most children wear a sweater at school, but take it off when they go out in the sun at recess. They're a little backward by Canadian standards. This makes Bill's job somewhat harder.

That's all for now. Love from,
Bill, Marg, Jeff, Linda, David.

P.S. Geckos don't really suck your blood, D--. They bite your nose!

Feb 1/71

Dear G--, P--, S-- & G--

Hi everyone! How's the weather over there? Not too cold I hope. Bill says thank you very much for the birthday card.

I'm afraid I can't help you too much with toilet training advice. Neither Jeff nor David were too dependable that way until they turned 3 years old. Linda was quite good by the time she was 1½ so I don't think it was anything I did. Just keep trying but don't worry about it - you've never seen a 20 yr. old in diapers.

Linda has started taking Indian dancing lessons. One of the Indian ladies in the Township is a dancer and she has consented to teach the girls. Linda had to be talked into going but she just loved the first lesson and can't wait for the next. They are going to learn Rajasthani dances so that should be something interesting to show when we get home. They have to get ankle bells and later will get Rajasthani outfits, which is a long gathered skirt and short blouse and lots of bangles.

Oh by the way Linda says that when you have your next child would you please make it a girl[23]. She is actually going to feel out of place when she gets with all her cousins.

Bye for now. Love to all,

Bill & Marg
Jeff, Linda & David

---

23  As luck would have it, that was indeed what happened.

## Why So Long?

We bet you've been asking yourself what happened to Bill & Marg? Or maybe you've just forgotten all about us since we haven't written for quite a long time. Anyway there are at least 8 reasons why this letter has been delayed and they follow in this newsletter so here goes...

## The Tranters' Beautiful New Car

Outside in our carport right now there sits a beautiful 1971 Westfalia Campmobile Volkswagen Van. It shines in the light of the garage bulbs and shimmers in the moonlight when driven at night. It has 800 miles on it already and is in perfect condition. Today Bill changed the oil in the crankcase and transmission, reinstalled an electric fan and spent at least 6 hours washing off the last remnants of shipping grease with kerosene, then washing off the kerosene with soap and water, then washing off the soap and water with the hose (actually the Mali did that) and then giving the whole car a good coat of wax. The beautiful white paint and chrome fittings are undoubtedly the pride of the community (even if there are 3 others the same here).

Just a short sidelight on cars in India. India manufactures two kinds of cars locally: an Ambassador (which looks like about a small 1952 English car) and a Fiat which is just a little bigger but still small by Canadian standards. They sell new for about Rs. 25,000 (which is about $3,500.00) and they look very old-fashioned and poorly made. There is a waiting list of several years for potential car buyers because the manufacturers cannot keep up with the demand of the few rich Indians that can afford to buy them. Imported cars are not allowed for sale in the country. An official of D.A.E. told us that if we could sell our car, there are Indians that would be willing to pay between 100,000 and 200,000 rupees for it (somewhere between 15,000 and 30,000 dollars). So you can imagine how rich we feel with a car worth almost 2 lakhs rupees (A lakh is an Indian numerical term meaning 100,000. There are also Crores which are worth 100 lakhs or 10,000,000).

Cars are so scarce and hard to buy in India that they are kept on the road long after a Canadian would have sent them to the junkyard. Every time we go to Kota we see cars in the city that could literally be sold as antiques in Canada! Some Indians are still driving cars that were built in the 1930's! It's unbelievable.

In case you don't remember what our car is like a short description follows. It is a white Volkswagen Van (truck) with a roof that raises at one end to allow more head room inside when camping. Inside there are seats for five (comfortably) plus a sink with running water, an ice box, collapsible beds for the whole family, lights, auxiliary heating system (really useful in India, ha, ha), dining table and half a dozen storage compartments for clothing, food, camping supplies, etc. It is available with a tent that attaches to the big side door but we don't have the tent. We'll buy that if we ever get back to Canada with it in one piece.

Our Trip to Bombay

We received word on February 3rd that the cars had arrived and been cleared through customs in Bombay. We left on Thursday, Feb 4th in the afternoon for Kota Train station without any reservations. After half an hour of being "chummy" with the local station master our names and those of the C--s (more Canadians going to get their car) mysteriously moved to the top of the waiting list for Air Conditioned seats on the Frontier Mail Train to Bombay. (It is surprising how effective an influence the "rich white sahibs" can have if they go out of their way to be friendly with local officials. Of course our open friendliness increases the local station master's status with all his employees too.)

The train trip to Bombay was uneventful. We got on the train at about 4:30 p.m. (An air conditioned compartment that sleeps four for the two couples.) We spent most of the evening talking to two Indian representatives of Johnson & Johnson who were returning to Bombay on a business trip. One had visited Canada and the other had friends there so they were most interested in visiting with us for the evening. The train arrived in Bombay at around 10:30 a.m. on Friday. We took a taxi to the West End Hotel and began making plans to pick up the cars. Most of Friday was spent fiddling around at D.A.E. getting the clearance of the cars all straightened out and with Bill ordering school supplies. Saturday was spent shopping and getting the cars properly serviced. We visited two interesting places in Bombay.

One was a lovely little restaurant called the "Bullock Cart". It featured discotheque music and a surprisingly varied menu of excellent food. We had a very enjoyable evening out there with the C—s. Following this we got a taxi driver to take us to the "Street of Cages". This street is famous around the world as a centre of licensed prostitution. There are literally hundreds of girls of every age, colour and size waiting to be propositioned. They are licensed and recognized by the government. We had our taxi driver drive us slowly along several streets while we stared out of the taxi windows at 10:30 p.m. on a Saturday night. Some girls walked along the sidewalk. Some were in little open front rooms with cage-type doors on the front (the reason for the name). Some places there were balconies with girls hanging over inviting passers-by to come up and see them. The taxi driver gave us a running commentary on the best houses (each place is numbered according to their government license). He explained that the cost of the girls' services varies from 3 to 5 rupees (40¢ to 75¢). Of course, he explained, there were much more expensive girls, but not on the street of cages. Whenever he offered to stop the cab, both Margaret and C-- C-- would yell and tell him to keep driving on. He thought it was a huge joke.

Another interesting place to see in Bombay is Crawford Market. If you can imagine St. Lawrence Market[24] increased about 4 times in size, you may have some idea of what this food market is like. There are booths and stalls selling every possible variety of fruits, vegetables, meat, spices, toys, tools, drugs, etc. There is a pet market that sells monkeys, parrots, half a dozen other kinds of birds, dogs, cats, tropical fish, etc. There are also fairly elaborate booths set up much like small grocery stores at home. We bought quite a large quantity of refined sugar and flour plus some nice fruits – oranges, grapefruits and pineapples. Although some of these items are available locally, the Bombay prices were low enough to make bringing back several hundred pounds of sugar and flour worthwhile. One thing is different in Crawford Market than in Canada. As soon as you arrive, you are besieged by "market boys", who are there to carry your shopping basket for you and show you where to buy anything you want. They will advise you and carry all your groceries for several hours for 1 rupee (15¢). E-- C-- and Bill were told you could buy anything in Crawford Market so they thought they would see if this was really true. They asked about buying imported liquor and even though it is strictly forbidden as an import item, there was soon a man offering to sell them Vat 69 whisky for 100 rupees ($14.00) a bottle on the black market. Of course, they didn't buy any at that price, but it was interesting to see that it is available. You just have to be willing to pay the price.

The Trip From Bombay

Sunday morning we left the hotel at around 6:30 a.m. and made another short stop at Crawford Market for blocks of ice (for the van ice-box) and pop. Then we started on the 700 mile trip by road from Bombay to Township. The main road which goes from Bombay all the way to Delhi was quite good. Of course it was bumpy by Canadian highway standards but it is paved all – or almost all – the way. It is also narrow by Canadian standards being only two lanes wide at the widest and often only one lane wide.

---

24　A large indoor public market in Toronto, Canada.

The scenery on the first part of the trip was most interesting. When you leave Bombay you climb through the hills (called Ghats) up to a central plateau region which covers most of central India. Part of the trip through the ghats looked much like the rocky mountains with the highway cut right out of the side of the cliff and train tracks coming out of tunnels through the mountains. Other parts were almost semi-desert at this time of year. There were many villages and towns along the way. One of the most tiring parts of the drive is the trucks. Being old and Indian they travel at an average speed of around 30 miles per hour (50 kilometres per hour for those of us in India using the Metric system). Since the road is narrow it is often difficult to get past. We found though that most drivers were helpful and would pull over to let you by at the first reasonable opportunity.

Thanks to getting slightly lost (have you ever tried to read Hindi road signs?) and to our fairly low average speed we arrived at Indore at 9:30 p.m. on Sunday. We stayed at the Lantern Hotel. When we arrived and asked to see our rooms we were shocked. The rooms they showed us were old, dirty, musty with concrete floors and partly painted walls. We said these rooms wouldn't do and asked if they had something better. After some rushing around we were shown the "V.I.P. Suite". A bedroom, dining room, lounge combination, fully carpeted with carved pillars, two lovely beds and a large tiled, clean bathroom. The C——s were also shown a better room but not quite as elaborate as ours. We had dinner served in our room by a very friendly but dirty room service boy. The food was just edible but we were tired and not feeling very appreciative at the time. In fact we all got feeling pretty silly and spent about half an hour trying to keep a straight face every time our room service boy returned with another course in our dinner with his filthy jacket and dirty, open toe running shoes.

We left the beautiful Lantern Hotel around 10:30 a.m. on Monday and took our time coming the last 300 miles home. The scenery in Rajasthan was some of the nicest we saw anywhere and there are several interesting towns we've made a note to go back and see again. We arrived home around 6:30 p.m. on Monday night tired but happy to have our "wheels" again.

## ANUSHAKTI "LAUGH-IN" 1971

In case you don't know, "Anushakti" is the Hindi name for the Atomic Reactor that is being built near township. This year, following a tradition begun last year, a variety show entitled "Anushakti Laugh-In[25], 1971" was held. Plans for this show began way back in December. Bill volunteered to help write scripts and ended up as the major script writer of the production and also one of the performers. The show was presented to an audience of Canadians and Indians (who travelled from as far as Delhi and Bombay to see it) on the evenings of February 12th and 13th). Admission price was 1 rupee for adults and free for children. Both nights there was a capacity audience of 300 people. The show lasted almost 3 hours and was a variety of songs, dances, skits and stunts designed to entertain and amuse people. Here is a summary of the skits written by Bill:

An interview with Jose Gecko (a human-size gecko lizard).

A song parody called "Tomorrow" based on the fact that all the local serviceman promise to come back tomorrow to finish their work and never do.

A song called "We're the wives of the motorcycle riders" sung by four local girls on two motorcycles.

A skit called "the bridge game" about 3 bridge players who are bothered by a fourth who doesn't know how to play.

A skit called "the Kota Guards" about the local army personnel planning a fantastic war manoeuvre that turns out to be a trip to R.A.P.P. Township to play water polo against the Canadians.

A 25-minute "drama" entitled "The R.A.P.P. Ranger meets Moti the Dhoti". A full-fledged production starring the R.A.P.P Ranger, his faithful Indian friend, Shonto, the hero Moti, the villain Rotten Raj (played by Bill) and the heroine Lulubelle. This was the culmination of the whole show.

There were many other items in the show too. Bill played in the Jose Gecko skit as a radio interviewer, as a customs inspection

---

25  The name was inspired by the popular American television comedy program called Laugh-In that aired from 1968 to 1973.

officer teaching young recruits how to "unpack" a shipment of household goods (also written by Bill), as a Rajasthani Water Girl in a dance in which 6 men poured pots of water on each other in time to Indian music, as a beautiful ballet dancer and can-can dancer in two other all-male dancing numbers and as mentioned above Rotten Raj.

The whole show was a great success under the fine direction of a local A.E.C.L. employee who unfortunately is leaving to go home to Toronto next week. Probably Bill and another Canadian who did a lot of the planning will take on the planning and organization of the whole show next year.

As you can imagine, though, putting on a 3-hour variety show is a lot of work and with rehearsals and lines to learn there hasn't been much time for the more mundane things of life like writing letters home. Just to add to the problem, Bill was sick for 3 days after coming home from Bombay. He came home the night of the dress rehearsal with a temperature of 103°. He even had a day off school!

### VALENTINES'S DANCE

Sunday, Feb. 14th was the Township Valentine's Dance. The dance band from Delhi was brought down and a swinging dance was held from 9:00 p.m. until all hours of the morning. We were one of the first to leave at around 1:00 am. The party was sponsored by several Canadians who are leaving in a few weeks as a final good-bye from them.

### INDIAN DRIVER'S LICENSES

Just as in Canada, in India you are <u>supposed</u> to have a driver's license. Recently a new police chief was appointed in Kota. He seemed to take great joy in trying to stop Canadians (and other foreigners) to check on their license. So most township residents decided it would be a good idea to get one. Upon inquiring, it was found that the driving tester from Chittorgargh Division (R.A.P.P. Township area) would come out on Saturday, Feb 13th to test people for an Indian driver's license. The test had two parts. First you had to prove you could identify Indian road signs (which have no words on them because lots of Indian drivers are illiterate). Then you had to take a practical test in driving too. In fact Bill had to take a driver's test and a motorcycle driver's test. Anyway, we passed the tests and were supposed to get our licenses next week but they haven't come yet. Some helpful suggestions offered by the driving instructor:

1. Never look back when you are backing up. Just use your rear-view mirrors.
2. When asked what he would do if he were stalled on a railway track when a train was coming, one Canadian said he would get out and run. The instructor said that was the wrong answer.
3. Part of the test was to show how slow you could drive in case you got behind a cripple on the road and couldn't get past him.

4. The motorcycle driving test was also a test of how slow you could go and how tight a circle you could make. Nobody taking the motorcycle test got out of low gear!

After testing all the people it was obvious that the instructor wasn't keeping track of whom he had tested and had no idea who he was testing during the road tests. When the D.A.E. coordinator came up to the house afterwards to collect the license fee, we gave him the fees for 2 car licenses and 2 motorcycle licenses so that Margaret will get a motorcycle driver's licenses even if she has only been on the motorcycle twice by herself. She can always frame it - or learn how to drive the motorcycle.

SLIDE-O-RAMA PARTY
On Sunday, February 21, 3 families in Township, the R—s, the G—s and the Tranter's organized a party in which there was a half-hour slide show showing funny slides taken mainly at crazy parties in Township, then about 3/4's of an hour of presentations to 3 families that are leaving soon. One lady got a certificate for playing 1,000 hours of bridge. She also got an Indian Housekeeping kit including all sorts of useful mementos like: an Indian broom, Indian floor rags, perfume called "Essence of Rawat Bhata (nearby village), unboiled water, sample of monsoon mud, etc., etc.
The next presentations were to her husband. He was the same man who directed the Anushakti Laugh-In so he received a director's chair covered with funny comments from the show, two tapes of the program taken during the show, as well as certificate for best-dressed man and an award for making the most speeches which interrupted parties.
The next awards went to another "star" in the variety show. He received the "Miss Rajasthani Water Pot Girl" award, an empty bottle of imported liqueur and, since he played the part of Jose Gecko in the show, a box of real live Geckos! That was really fun. You should have heard the women scream when three geckos came jumping out of the box heading for the walls. One of the geckos was actually quite friendly and stayed on his arm for 3 or 4 minutes before running off to hide.
The last presentations were to the G—s who have been transferred to Bombay. Mrs G— got an award for playing bridge. Mr. G— got a trophy for waiting longer for his imported car than anyone else (11 months!). Then they were both given a Bombay survival kit including all sorts of crazy items like a Bombay cockroach killer (big hand on a long stick), Bombay taxi hailer (big hand on a long stick), and many other items. We thought up most of the crazy presentations and everyone really seemed to enjoy them. Then the party went on with dancing, talking, etc. until about 1:30 a.m.

Father & Son Banquet
Yesterday, (Monday, 22nd) there was a special Scouting program at the school after 4:00 p.m. in which Indian cubs, scouts, brownies

and guides met with Canadians in township with a program of songs, dances, etc. It was very well attended and the program, planned partly by E-- W-- and partly by the Indian Leaders, was very good.

The program was followed at 6:30 p.m. by a Father & Son banquet in which Bill, Jeff and David attended. We had a nice meal of fried chicken, vegetables, scalloped potatoes, apple pie and coffee (or pop). Then we enjoyed a short program of speeches, songs, skits and a Rajasthani folk dance by six young Bulbuls (brownies) from the Indian pack. By the way, David was enrolled as a cub last Saturday so now we have two cubs and a brownie in our family.

## CASINO NIGHT

Last night (Monday, again) was also the night of another party. Two families were celebrating (?) being here exactly a year. They decided to do it by having a party with all kinds of gambling games for people to play. Bill printed up some money for them and it was sold at the door. (The average bill used for gambling was worth 10 paise – 1½ cents). Games included roulette, Michigan Rummy, Rummoli, dice, darts and bridge and Euchre. Bill spent most of the night acting as a croupier in the roulette game but also played roulette, darts, etc. Margaret had a very enjoyable game of Rummoli and managed to lose some of Bill's winnings at the roulette wheel. We ended up losing about 3 rupees (45¢) after a night of fun that started for us at 9:30 p.m. and ended at about 1:30 a.m. (again!)

## OUR FIRST TRIP

Well, enough about the past. We are planning our first big car trip with the van on the second week of March (the school Winter Holiday break). We are going to drive to Jaipur and spend two days there. Then we go on to Delhi for about 3 days. Then drive to Agra to see the Taj Mahal. We hope to get lots of pictures. Of course we're taking the children. We have written away for hotel reservations but if we really get stuck we could always sleep in the van. Actually the trip should be most enjoyable. The road is supposed to be quite good. None of the trips from one place to another will take more than half a day.

We are looking forward to seeing more of Jaipur (and staying in the palace again). We hope to do more shopping in Old Delhi this time and see more sights including the Red Fort. In Agra, of course, the main attraction is the Taj Mahal. It will be close to full moon, so we'll try to get some slides of the Taj Mahal by moonlight as well.

## A Record

Well, this letter probably sets two records. One for the longest you've had to wait for one - over 3 weeks. Another for the longest newsletter we have ever written. It has taken 2 hours of solid typing to complete it and since it's 11:30 p.m. we'll close for the night.

By the way, we hope you pity us for the hard life we lead here in this deserted little stretch of Rajasthan. It really is a tough life so far away from civilization. Why, some week's there's a week night with nothing to do! It's terrible! So boring! So take pity on us and write often. It gives us something to do in our spare time – reading letters that is. And we'll try to get the next one out in less time than the last one. Good-bye for now. Don't forget to write soon.

Love from,
Margaret, Bill, Jeff, Linda & David.
R.A.P.P. Township,
India.

## A Special Day

Margaret has just reminded me that we have been in R.A.P.P Township exactly 8 months today! What a thrill for you people back in Canada to know such important facts! We've been in India almost 9 months - no that's wrong - we've been away from Canada almost 9 months, but that includes the time spent on our European tour on the way over.

## Weather

We are all glad to hear that spring has come to Canada. Spring sprang here quite a while ago. We just checked the temperature outside - it is 9:45 p.m. and the temperature outside is 91 degrees. Inside it's about 95 degrees. Of course, the temperature is much lower in the two bedrooms we are using. There is an air conditioner in each room. We have all the children sleeping in the same bedroom now so they can all benefit from the air conditioner. The ceiling fans are going all the time too. They provide really good circulation of air.

Actually, even though the temperature is in the high nineties in the shade every day, you seldom feel any perspiration. The air is so dry that it evaporates almost instantly. They say it's not the heat, it's the humidity. There's a lot of truth in that. This dry heat is not very uncomfortable at all. Of course, it helps to have air conditioners, forced air cooling in the school and a handy Olympic sized swimming pool (which we use every day, of course!) Have you been swimming much in Canada yet? We swim every night from about 4:30 p.m. until 6:00. It's really quite nice. You should try it.

## Our Recent Trip

In our last letter we told you we were going to go to Jaipur, New Delhi and Agra. Well, we did it. So here's a little news about our experiences.

## Jaipur

We left on the Saturday morning, March 13th, at around 8:30 a.m. We travelled with another Canadian family, the C--s, who also have a Volkswagen Camping Van. Our first stop was on the way to Kota. Our interest was attracted by dozens and dozens of vultures circling around the side of the road. We stopped to find no less than three dead water buffalo in three different spots near the side of the road. We got out and spent almost half an hour taking gory movie film and colour slides of wild dogs and vultures eating the dead water buffalo. The films have been sent back to Canada a week and a half ago. So you may see them very soon if you haven't already - along with a lot of other things we did on the trip (2 reels). However, don't watch this one right after a big meal. We arrived in Jaipur, the pink city, around the middle of the afternoon after stopping under a banyan tree for lunch at noon. When we first stopped it was deserted. By the time we had finished lunch, half the men from the nearby village were there sitting around, watching us and generally acting friendly but curious. I used the opportunity to cross the road and take some pictures of a well from which water was drawn by two oxen. This is the most common kind of irrigation well found in the part of India we have seen. They are all over the place so we got some movie footage of that too.

In Jaipur, we stayed at the Rambagh Palace Hotel again – the old palace of the Maharajah of Jaipur. It was very nice, though the food isn't wonderful. While we were there, we did quite a bit of shopping for: a chess set for Bill, some jewellery, brassware, etc. We saw the Jaipur zoo, a carpet factory in which almost all of the carpet weaving is done by boys between 6 and 12 years of age - the carpets are beautiful. We saw a lovely embossed carpet – 9x12 – in dark blue that was made there. It cost about 2,200 Rupees ($300.00). We didn't buy it though. It probably wouldn't look right in Canada even if it would be worth a great deal more.

We spent one interesting afternoon at the Rambagh Palace. On the grounds there is an enclosed pool which was originally used by the Maharajah. Since it was for his private enjoyment, the pool is equipped with a slide going into the water, two diving boards, two sets of rings suspended on ropes from the ceiling over the middle of the pool, two trapeze swings set up the same way, etc. The kids thought it was just great playing Tarzan – holding onto a ring at the side and swinging out over the water, then letting go. Lots of fun. The water was cold – temperature in the pool must have been in the high sixties but it was worth suffering the cold water for the fun we had.

Delhi

We left Jaipur on Monday morning for Delhi. The drive took us through a lot of semi-desert country. We crossed a number of rivers that were just sand flowing under a bridge. Yet we were impressed by the number of places where a little bit of water had been dispersed through irrigation ditches to grow crops where you would never expect crops to grow. The road to Delhi was quite decent by Indian standards although only two fairly narrow lanes wide at its widest points.

We arrived in Delhi around 3:00 p.m. and went to the Claridges Hotel. There we were told that unfortunately, there were no double rooms large enough to fit in the three extra beds and would we take a "luxury suite" at the same price? We agreed and found that a luxury suite includes an immense bedroom - with room for five beds, a writing desk and still lots of space, a separate fully furnished living room and another separate furnished dining room with its own refrigerator, buffet, etc. It was rather luxurious so we made the best of it. Of course, we swam in the hotel pool - outdoors, but certainly nice and had several good meals in the hotel dining room. The children - our 3 and the C--'s 2 - had dinner one evening in our hotel suite dining room served every course by a most pleasant and gracious waiter. Our children are certainly learning to live like rich people - at least when they leave township!

While in Delhi we saw the Red Fort - a huge red sandstone building that was the seat of government for India during the Moghul reign and for part of the British rule of India. We saw the parliament buildings, we took a trip though old Delhi with the car and drove about three-quarters of an hour one night through streets so narrow and crowded that the car almost touched the buildings on both sides. We also took a trip through the International Doll Museum where there are dolls displayed from countries around the world and visited the Children's Library and Reading Room where there is a display of thousands of titles of children's books all freely available for any child to come and sit down to read. Of course we went shopping in Delhi too and we bought a few souvenirs and items we needed. The Indian election returns were just coming in the day before we left. Of course there are few Indians that have television so instead crowds gather in front of the large press buildings and the latest results were chalked up minute by minute. There were thousands watching the results. We stayed long enough to see that Indira Gandhi had a good majority coming along. We were glad of that. It ensures a reasonably quiet future in India with a minimum of rioting, etc.

Agra

We left Thursday morning for Agra. The road from Delhi to Agra is probably the best in India - much of it is 4-lane divided highway. You can actually go over 60 miles an hour in places - wow! Again we stopped in the shade of a tree for lunch and as we ate we were visited and viewed by a mother and her two children. Before we left we offered them some cheese sandwiches, cookies, etc. and the mother accepted them readily for her children but when Bill tried to take a picture of one of her children she refused to allow it.

We arrived in Agra again around 3:00 in the afternoon and proceeded, rather indirectly, to the Clarke-Shiraz Hotel – a nice six-story modern hotel quite near to the Taj Mahal. The rooms were modern and bright like an American hotel or motel and it had the usual lobby with its handicraft shops, etc. The children were disappointed to learn that the swimming pool was not filled, but we decided we could probably survive for three days without it.

Written on the back: *This proves we were really there. M. Mar/71*

Of course our first trip out from the hotel was to the Taj Mahal. It is really beautiful. The building is a little larger than I expected and the grounds are somewhat smaller. Pictures give you a false impression of distances. Actually the Taj Mahal and its grounds are all inside a walled in area with a beautiful red sandstone gate leading in. It is only when you step through the gate that you see the scene of the Taj Mahal that every book and travel folder has. The building is absolutely perfectly balanced – each side being a perfect mirror image of the other side. Inside the walls, tombs, etc. are covered with inlaid gems and semi-precious stones. The amount of work involved is immense. It was easy to see why it took 20,000 workers 22 years to build it. Of course we took pictures – movie film, slides and black and white film (see the shot enclosed). During our three-day stay in Agra we went back to the Taj Mahal three times to see it at different times of the day or to see different parts of it. Bill and E-- C-- went back at 10:30 p.m. one night with cameras, tripod, cable release, etc. to take shots of the Taj Mahal by moonlight. We haven't got the slides back yet so we don't know if they turned out.

Written on the back: Here *is a picture to show the reflection of the Taj Mahal in the pool. Remember G--, you said that's what you wanted to see. Mar./71*

As well as the Taj Mahal, we took a trip out to an abandoned city about 22 miles from Agra called Fatepur Sikri. This city was built in lavish style and used for just 22 years and then abandoned because of the lack of sufficient drinking water. There was a beautiful small marble tomb there equal in workmanship to the Taj Mahal but of course much smaller plus a number of other interesting buildings and people. Unfortunately most of the people there now are tourist vendors selling every possible tourist souvenir. The children had fun bargaining with some for a couple of rupees. Friday in Agra was Holi – a Hindu festival in which Indians celebrate by throwing paint or coloured water at everyone in the streets. People staying at the hotel were advised to stay in on Friday and we did. Several of the sons of Canadians also staying at the hotel ventured outside the hotel grounds and came back spattered in paint. Of course we would have been spattered much worse if we had spent the day in township. It is always a wild time with everyone throwing coloured water at everyone else. Next year we'll have to stay around and let the children join in the fun.

Saturday morning we left to come home. We went south from Agra through Gwalior and Shivpuri[26] – an area known as dacoit country. In case you didn't know, dacoits are highway robbers or bandits which are pretty common in parts of India. Often they are retired military personnel or other trained fighters. They are often well supplied with guns and ammunition and raid villages stealing goods and holding villagers for ransom. They also stop cars on the highway occasionally and rob people. We didn't see any signs of them. However, we read in the paper that on the Monday following our trip through Gwalior (on Saturday) one villager was killed by dacoits and there was quite a fight between a group of villagers and dacoits. After we left Shivpuri we travelled for 120 miles along an absolutely terrible road which ranged from one-lane paved to completely broken up. I doubted if we averaged 15 miles an hour over parts. Our overall average for the 120 miles must have been less than 30 miles per hour. We finally arrived home around 7:30 p.m. tired but pleased with our trip. The car ran very well and we had seen a lot of India.

Written on the back: *Ready to go after a picnic lunch on the road from Agra. March, 1971*

A Sunday Excursion

On Sunday, Bill was asked to lead an excursion of three Volkswagen vans through an overland area to some caves he had visited two weeks before with the cub pack. There were three visitors in township from A.E.C.L. and Hydro. The excursion was planned to give them a look at India uninfluenced by the Canadians in R.A.P.P. Township. The three vans forded a stream and followed a back road – mainly dirt and rocks for about five miles. Then they left the road and travelled overland to the edge of a cliff. Down the carved steps beside the cliff were two caves. One is a Hindu shrine of worship. The other is just a shallow cave. The visitors were quite interested.

---

26  Now known as Kundeshwar Dham.

On the way back, we lost our way overland and weren't sure what direction to go. Everybody in the excursion - about 15 people - had a different idea. Fortunately, we soon met up with three Rajasthan police constables and a camel who offered to show us the way. They got in the vans and did show us the way - but not the way we had come! The road back included unbelievably rough areas including one section of the road - if you could call it a road - which was a stream with a foot of mud on the bottom. The vans went through absolutely everything. All three drivers were really pleased at their performance. We all agreed that if we could have made a 16 m.m. movie of that trip Volkswagen would have probably bought it for quite a large sum.

Finally we came out at the Indian village we were using as a road mark. There we were met by a large group of celebrating villagers including a drummer and two bagpipe players. (Did you know that Indian villagers often have pipers?) We were invited to meet the groom - or proposed groom for a wedding that was being celebrated in the community. The bride was some distance away in a neighbouring village but we could meet the groom. He was a boy of about 12 who seemed rather shy and overwhelmed at all the attention he was getting. We presented him with a wedding present of about 10 rupees which seemed to please everyone. Then we got back in the vans and came home. You wouldn't believe the sight our car was after travelling over those dusty roads! It was a real mess inside and out. The first thing Bill did when he got home was go down for a swim and get rid of all the dust. At least the visitors were most pleased to have seen the caves, to be lost on an overland trip in India and to see an unspoiled rural Indian village.


Plans for the Summer

At present, we hope to go to Kashmir for the month of June. We'll see the Himalayas and see a part of India that is cool and comfortable when township is over 100 degrees almost every day. We've sent away for information and received it so now we just have to get the reservations we want. We hope we'll be able to get them, but more information about that in future newsletters.

As usual, everyone is well and happy. School is going quite well. There are no holidays until it ends at the end of May so the kids are working hard to finish up their school year. An "Open House" is planned for the week after next when parents can come and see their children's school work. School is taking up a lot of Bill's time. This is the time of year when reports and requests for supplies must be sent to Canada if we are to get them next year. So he is keeping very busy in the evenings as well. We are also organizing a community paperback library at the school so that members of the community can donate paperbacks and come in and withdraw more that they haven't read - at least for the lazy Canadian women with their cooks, gardeners, sweepers and ayahs (babysitters).

Well, that's about all for now. Please write soon. We enjoy your letters.

                    Love,
                    Marg, Bill, Jeff, Linda and David.

What's New:

Well, brace yourself for another wild, exciting, stimulating letter from India. Actually, you don't have to brace yourself too much. The last few weeks have been rather dull so we'll use this opportunity to get you up to date on some of the dreary day-to-day routine of life in Township.

A Typical Week:

We thought we'd start by describing the highlights of a typical week in R.A.P.P. Township. It starts last Saturday and goes until today - Friday.

Saturday, April 10th - Left at 9:00 a.m. with one of the Canadian Engineers for a tour of the Atomic Power Plant Project. Margaret, Bill and Linda going. The boys are at cubs. Drove out and spent 2½ hours touring the plant. Things are moving along pretty well. The plant should go critical (begin a controlled atomic reaction) sometime early in 1972. Of course, that won't end the project because two plants are being built at the site and the second will take another couple of years to complete. The piping and electrical wiring is incredibly complicated but very impressive looking.

When we returned, the boys were pleased because they had got a new Canadian Cub handbook full of great ideas, projects, etc.

We spent the afternoon at the pool.

We invited our friends, the C-—s, for supper. They took their kids home and returned to play Milles Bournes until around midnight. Our menu for supper? Chicken pilau (an Indian mixture of rice, small french fries, chicken, raisins, carrots, peas, etc. plus a mild curry sauce.), tossed salad, papadum (looks like a great big potato chip - very thin and deep fried instead of bread).
For dessert: a Duncan Hines cake and ice cream (chocolate or vanilla).
Also: a bottle of still rose wine brought by the C-—s (Indian and not too bad - Indian wines are generally poor and expensive!)

Sunday - children and Margaret attended Sunday School on Easter Sunday as they do every Sunday. Spent the afternoon at the pool. Bill worked on school work in the evening - reports due to go out on Monday.

Monday - regular school day for all except Margaret. Progress Reports went out to all parents. Marg and Bill attended a party in the evening for the Canadian families leaving soon. Party was held outside in the back garden although it was really rather warm there. Spent the evening talking, visiting with people, etc. Quiet but good.

Tuesday - regular school day. In the evening Bill went down at 8:30 p.m. for his weekly games of volleyball. A grudge match between Ontario Hydro and the A.E.C.L.-M.E.C.O[27]. team saw the A.E.C.L.-M.E.C.O. team winner in every game. (Bill is A.E.C.L.) Bill passed up his usual late-night dip in the pool after volleyball. Instead came home and wrote letter to Kashmir finalizing our plans for a trip there in June.

Wednesday - regular school day. In the evening went to a PR party planned by Lufthansa Airlines - free food, drinks and prizes for Canadians in Township to publicize their air service to and from India. Marg and Bill each won 4 beer mugs with German coats-of-arms and Lufthansa on them. Other prizes were cut glass whisky glasses (Rosenthal), Lufthansa flight bags, luggage tags, lighters, etc. Left about 11:30 p.m.

Thursday - regular school day. Thursday night is movie night. This week it was Elvis Presley in "Live a Little, Love a Little". We decided that the makers should have added "Hate a Little" to fit in with the quality of the movie. It had lovely colour, etc. but the acting and story was Bad! Bad Bad! The kids thought it was good.

Friday - another typical school day. This evening we invited the W——s to dinner. They visited until around 9:15 p.m. while their 2 children played with our three. Now we're just writing this letter.

NOTE: I haven't told what Margaret does during the day. That's because she doesn't do anything except lie around reading and ordering the servants about between shopping trips, visits to girl friends and acting as an unofficial bus service for people temporarily without cars.

Another "Let's Feel Sorry for the Tranter's" Session:
In case you think our life is all fun and games listen to the following shocking events:
- In the last 2 weeks we have killed 3 poisonous Ginger Spiders outside our door just after dark. Linda almost put her hand on one when she was coming in. You know what Linda is like with spiders! She decided to come in the other way rather quickly! The ones we caught were rather small - only about 1-2 inches across including legs. The full-sized ones are almost as big as the palm of your hand with a very painful and possibly serious bite.

---

27  Montreal Engineering Company Ltd, one of the contractors working on the project.

- Lots of scorpions still around. A girl was bitten last Monday night. It was painful for several hours but there were no other ill effects.
- A number of poisonous (or allegedly poisonous) snakes have been killed in township in the past month. We killed one - non-poisonous.
- I stopped this letter 5 minutes ago to stamp on a cockroach. You remember cockroaches don't you? There are still lots in India. Many of them live in our refrigerator!
- Our house is infested with geckos - lizards 4-6 inches long that go around the walls pretending to eat insects. They don't really eat insects. They just hang around causing trouble, laying eggs in the drawers and leaving droppings on the walls and floor.
- The weather is now hot enough to have two fans and cooling systems (the Indian ones are called "cus-cus" going in the living room all day and have ceiling fans and air conditioners in the bedrooms going all night. Last night the power was off for several hours and Margaret had trouble sleeping because of the heat. I'll check the temperature outside right now at 10:30 p.m. after 3½ hours of darkness - 90 degrees. The last 2 days have been cooler than most. Yesterday was a big event. We saw a cloud in the sky! Wow! We almost took a picture of it. Of course it wouldn't be too exciting back in Canada.

- Pop - you know that Bill likes pop! Well here they sell pop too. You can buy Coca-Cola, Fanta Orange and Fanta soda water. Of course they have never heard of Freshie, Tang, etc. You can buy "squash" - a liquid drink syrup in orange, lemon and lime. There are several other unbearable flavours too but they are undrinkable. Most of the time we drink Coke and Fanta orange. When we get back to Canada we'll never drink Coke and Fanta again after so much of it here. What happened to ginger ale, lemon lime, grape, cream soda, etc. etc?

Well that should be enough to get you crying for a while. Maybe we'll give you some more "sob stories" next time.

Hindi Lessons
    The boys and girls at school are taking Hindi lessons now. For the past 2 weeks they've begun to develop their vocabulary with the help of our Indian Kindergarten teacher. Today the pupils in Bill's class put on a number of short skits in Hindi only containing such valuable phrases as:

Greetings, How much is the fruit? It is 2 rupees. I need 6 oranges. It costs 12 rupees. 2, 4, 6, 8, 10, 12. Thank you. etc. etc.

In case you want to impress your Hindi-speaking friends, here is a short vocabulary lesson:

Hello – *Namastay* (press palms together – fingers pointing up & bow slightly)

What is that – *Yuh kyuh hye?*

That is a chair – *Yuh kursi hye.*

I need some water – *Mujay pahnee chah-he-yay.*

Thank you – *Shukri-ya.*

So well we probably won't even remember English when we come back to Canada for the first few months. We'll be speaking all Hindi.[28]

Pool:

    The swimming pool is very nice. We go swimming every week night from 4:30 until almost 6:00 p.m. On weekends we spend a few hours there each day. We swim, dive, wrestle, play water basketball, have races, lie in the sun, talk, etc. It is nice to be able to swim for 7 or 8 months of the year instead of just for 3 or 4 at most. Of course, David, Linda and Jeff are all swimming well. David can dive (not jump) off the high board which is at least 10 feet above the water. (Can you?) They can spend literally hours fooling around in 9 – 10 feet depth of water.

Our Household Staff

    We've neglected to keep you up to date on our household staff. We have had a different cook for about a month and a half now. His name is Ross and he is an old and experienced cook. He is pretty good although his baked goods – bread, buns, cakes, etc. aren't always the best. Generally, though we are very pleased with him. Our former cook, Mary, is working down the hill at another Canadian home. We still have the same sweeper, Rosan, although she is beginning to look rather pregnant so she may soon be gone. We have a new part-time Mali (gardener) who works at our place for a few hours each day and sends his wife up at other times to do the watering. We still have a dhobi coming twice a week to do the ironing. Margaret, brave girl, still does the washing herself! How's that for unselfish effort?

---

28  Little did we know that where we lived in Ontario (Bramalea-Gore-Malton) would someday have the largest percentage of people of East Indian ethnic origin in Canada, currently over 40% of the population.

Music:

My guitar: I (Bill) am learning to play the guitar with the help of 3 different teach-yourself books plus 3 different records on how to play the guitar. Actually I'm quite pleased with my progress. I can play about 10 basic chords and quite a number of songs. The kids like to sing along. Margaret likes to leave the room. When we get home you are invited to a guitar-playing contest between me and D-- O-- another famous do-it-yourself guitar player. What a fantastically exciting event that will be!

Recorders: All pupils in R.A.P.P. township Canadian Elementary School take recorder lessons and like it! That is a school rule! Actually they are making excellent progress as the parents found out last week at our school Open House where, among other things, they heard the primary classes play such favourites as Twinkle Twinkle Little Star, Three Little Indians (American) and Puff the Magic Dragon. The senior classes played a number of more difficult one and two-part songs ending with quite a recognizable version of O Canada. The Open House was a real success. The parents are very pleased with the school program. They should be. It's one of the best offered anywhere in India. It is planned and administered by the highest-paid teacher in India bar none. Local Indian teachers only make 600 – 700 rupees a month ($100).

That's all for now! Good-bye from Marg, Bill, Jeff, Linda & David.

## What's New?

Things have been quiet around here for the last month or so -
particularly in the mail department! We seem to have received far
less letters than usual recently. We haven't decided whether this is
because:

1. Spring has come to Canada and everyone is too busy to write.
                    OR
2. Nobody has any news.
                    OR
3. Indian mails are slow for some reason. A number of our
neighbours have found the same thing so it may be delayed mails.
Although all letters received recently have taken the usual ten
days or so.

Anyway, we didn't feel left out in the mail department today - we got
a Christmas card! What a lovely surprise - when the temperature
outside is over a hundred!

## Weather

The weather is no different than it has been for the past 8
months except warmer. Each morning it is in the nineties. Each
afternoon it goes up to around 100 degrees. The children play outside
very little except to go to the pool. Games, Meccano sets, etc. are
getting heavy use at home. At school recess means moving to the next
room to play chess, play games on the blackboard or do jig-saw
puzzles. It is not uncommon to have to remind the pupils that it's
recess and they should stop their regular school work and take a
break.

## The Pool

The pool was closed Wednesday night to be drained, cleaned and
then refilled. They cleaned it quickly and it's being refilled - a 3-
day job. With luck we may be back in by Sunday afternoon. With such a
warm, sunny climate it is difficult to keep the pool clear of algae.
It was beginning to look a little murky and some dirt was
accumulating on the bottom so they emptied it.

The other day, David swam the width of the pool under water. He
still likes to remember his Uncle D-- calls him "shark".

## Volleyball

Monday night is volleyball night for some of the men in
township. They have played regularly on Monday nights for most of the
year. We usually get from 8 to 12 players out. Sometimes the women
come down to watch. With regular play we're getting pretty good. Some
points take a long time to win with the ball being volleyed across
the net many times before the point is scored. It's a lot of fun.
Since the weather has been quite warm, some of us finish the game

with a fast late swim in the pool before coming home. Very refreshing.

## Ginger Spiders

Do you know what Ginger spiders look like? We do. We see several every week outside or in our garage. They grow up to about 4 inches in diameter including legs and roar around looking for people to bite. We have killed at least 5 in the past month. So far all outside. Their bite is supposed to be painful but seldom fatal – lucky, eh?

## Margaret's Trip to the Hospital

Since this is Margaret's story, you will be pleased to know that she dictated this word for word to me (Bill). I have had a cyst on my shoulder for years and it got infected. I went to the doctor and he decided that it had better be removed. Last Friday, I went to the hospital and had it removed in the operating room under a local anaesthetic. It wasn't too bad but although you don't feel any pain you could certainly feel the pressure of him digging around. However, it's all healed up now and I am just waiting for the three stitches to dissolve like the doctor said they would.

The doctor who performed the "operation" was Doctor B--, an Indian surgeon who was trained in England and is highly respected by the Canadians. We've been here for nine months and I'm the first of our family to have to visit the hospital so we're doing pretty well. (End of Margaret's quote).

## Poor Bill, the Handyman

About two weeks ago my motorcycle had its first flat tire. Luckily it was the front wheel. It isn't as hard to remove as the back wheel. So, since the nearest tire repair service in a garage is 35 miles away (not counting the local unreliable tire-wallah) I had to fix it myself. Now I can thank Dad for letting me help him fix tires on our old cars when I was little. Remember tire irons? Remember patching kits? They are all needed here! The repair job was 100% successful.

On Saturday while parked in Kota I found I had a flat on the car. So we put on the spare and drove home. The tire had a triangle-shaped wedge of hard wood in it about 1½ inches long and ½ inch wide. I tried to repair that with my tubeless tire repair kits, but the hole is too big to get a completely air-tight seal so one of our tires with just a few thousand miles on it will now be used with a tube in it.

We don't intend to use it right away through. We'll use one of the 4 new tires I brought with the car. It means a trip to Kota again tomorrow though to have the tire changed and another tubeless tire put on the rim. How would you like to travel a 70-mile round trip to get a tire changed?

Just to finish off, on Wednesday I got a flat tire on the back of the motorcycle! So last night I took off the back wheel – a rotten job with all those gears, brakes, speedometer cables, etc. Then I struggled the tire off the rim – put a new tube in, struggled the tire back on again only to discover that the tube leaked and I would have to take the tire back off again and repair it.

"Oh phooey!" I said, "That is a hard job."

"Too bad" said Margaret with her fingers in her ears.

Anyway, when I got the tire back off I found that there was a slow leak due to some slight damage done by the tire iron as the tire was being put on before. After patching it, the tire was again put on the rim and the back wheel was put back together again on the motorcycle. You can imagine what I looked like after fooling around with it for two hours in the garage with a temperature of 95 degrees or more. Anyway, this time it stayed up and Margaret and I celebrated by driving to beautiful Rawat Bhata at about 10:30 p.m. just for a ride to try out the motorcycle.

Another Great Movie

We just came back from another of our great weekly movies. After starting almost an hour late, the whole family enjoyed "Rob Roy" that great Walt Disney feature about Scottish rebels. Of course, quite a bit of it was missing because any film that gets damaged by previous users is just cut out and of course the movie is about a hundred years old to start with but it was great fun! Wow! What excitement!

Holidays

We got a letter the other night confirming most of our reservations for our trip to Kashmir. Just 2½ weeks of school left until our holidays begin and then it's swimming, fishing, hiking and exploring the "wilds" of Kashmir!

## Brownie Mother and Daughter Banquet

A week ago Wednesday the Brownies had a Mother and Daughter Banquet up at the guest house. The food was provided by all the mothers bringing one main course and one dessert for a pot-luck supper. Linda was in several skits and in a semaphore demonstration. They also saw slides of Brownie activities and other township events such as the Anushakti Laugh-In. There are some excellent slides of the crazy show that was put on. We'll have to try to get some duplicates made for our slide collection.

## Closing

Well, that's all for now. Write soon. How's the weather in Canada? How are all the pets and children?

Love,
Bill, Marg, Jeff, Linda & David.

P.S. A big ha! ha! to all students and teachers who have to go to school to the end of June. Our last day is May 26th!

May 28th

Left R.A.P.P. Township for Delhi. Left house at about 7:00 a.m. with all the gear necessary for every possibility from camping to staying in posh hotels.

The first section of the drive – from Kota to Bundi – was frustrating because of the narrow roads and the great many ox-carts, bicycles, cows, etc. on the road. Average speed for this section must have been about 30 m.p.h.

After Bundi, the road cleared and widened a little and we arrived in Jaipur around 1:00 p.m. We stopped at Niro's – our favourite Jaipur restaurant for club sandwiches, hamburgers, iced tea and ice cream sundaes. The service was terrible. We didn't leave until after 2:00 p.m.

The next leg of our journey from Jaipur to Delhi was on good highway – two full lanes wide – and not too much traffic. The Indians have enough sense not to travel in the hot part of the day. We made good time and arrived at Claridges Hotel in Delhi at about 6:30 p.m. After a shower, we drove down to the main shopping centre and looked through the shops. Then we returned and had supper around 8:30 p.m.

May 29th-31st

We spent these four days in Delhi shopping, exploring in the car, resting up and buying some supplies needed for our trip. Bill spent one whole day having the car serviced and having the spare tire bracket installed on the front. Sunday was a lost day for shopping because all the stores are closed. Monday we finished shopping and got the car repacked for an early start on Tuesday.

June 1st

Left Delhi for Jammu at around 6:45 a.m. The road from Delhi to Jammu is excellent – good and wide and well-paved. It was a long drive though with interruptions for lunch and at least one town where we were almost lost – definitely confused for 15 or 20 minutes. We also were <u>hit</u> by a pedestrian. While travelling through a fairly busy main drag of a town at around 15-20 m.p.h. a man came running out from the side of the road with a sack of something on his head. He didn't look ahead at all – in fact he couldn't see because of the sack. He ran right into the side of the car near the back. His load was knocked off his head by the momentum of the car and he fell on the road. We slowed – wondering whether to stop or not. But he stood up again immediately and seemed all right so we kept going, not wanting to risk either an angry crowd or a legal investigation with some unreliable witnesses.

---

29  Handwritten at the top of the letter: "Please excuse all the typographical errors. The electric power on the houseboat is quite low tonight and Bill can't really see what he is doing."

We arrived in Jammu shortly after crossing the Jammu & Kashmir border where we had to show our passports and pay a toll of Rs. 2.50. Jammu is a small Indian city with the usual smells and poverty. We had reservations at the newly built Tourist Reception Centre. We had two double rooms. The rooms were clean but simply furnished. The walls were painted poured concrete and the bathroom was bare of any paint with a toilet, a stand-up shower and a sink, In spite of such lacks as no toilet paper (Indians use a cup of water) we had hot water, air conditioners in each room, comfortable beds, etc. Total cost for the two rooms was about $8.00 for the night. There was a restaurant and bar attached. The restaurant served mainly Indian food so we ordered Chicken pilau - a mixture of rice, spices and chicken. It was quite good though rather plain compared to our own cook's recipes. Jeff & Linda had chicken sandwiches, chips and Cokes. David shared the chicken pilau with us.

June 2nd

After a breakfast of toast and coffee - no juice, the toast was buttered with rancid butter and the coffee was do-it-yourself instant - we left for what we thought would be a short, interesting drive to Srinagar. It turned out to be interesting, but not short!

The road signs in Jammu said that the distance to Srinigar is about 280 kilometres (190 miles). What they didn't tell you was that it was almost 200 miles of twisting, turning, climbing road up and down through the mountains. For most of the trip we were lucky to average 20-25 m.p.h. because of the steep inclines on the road, the difficulty in passing slow trucks, buses, etc. and the extreme curves.

The country was beautiful but the driving was tough - around roads that hang out over the edge of mountains, over bridges that look down hundreds of feet to river valleys below, through villages perched on the side of the mountains. It was an unforgettable ride. Several things were particularly impressive. At different points along the road they have plaques and monuments commemorating men who died when their car went over the side. This road was built primarily as a military road to get troops up to Kashmir during the Indo-Pakistan border war of a few years ago. The plaques read something like this:

"In commemoration of our beloved leader, Major So-and-so,
who died when his jeep went out of control over this ledge.
May 15th, 1949."

Very inspiring feeling as you can imagine.

Another memorable spot was "J-Tunnel". At the highest point on the road when it has to cross a mountain peak, a tunnel has been built for a mile and a quarter through the mountain instead of over top of it. There are actually 2 separate tunnels side-by-side with stop lights at both ends. When you get the green light you drive through a tunnel that must be in some places at least a mile under the rock. It's just like driving your car through a well-paved but poorly lighted mine shaft.

After passing through "J-Tunnel" we went down into the Kashmir Valley (the famed "Vale of Kashmir") and the road straightened out for the last 50 miles into a long stretch of good highway. On both sides there were underwater rice paddies. The road seemed almost like a causeway going through the middle of the fields.

We arrived in Srinigar around 6:30 p.m. and after a small amount of driving around, located the Tourist Bureau. In the parking lot we were met by the owner of the houseboat we had rented. We were also met by at least 10 other men who wanted to rent us their houseboats. After checking on our houseboat owner's credentials in the Tourist Office he got in the car and directed us to the main dock on Dal Lake where we parked the car and proceeded with our luggage by shikara to our houseboat.

A shikara is a flat-bottomed gondola-like boat about 20 feet long with padded seats for the passengers - us. It only holds about 5 or 6 people and is paddled or poled along the lake. It has a woven grass roof and colourful material on the low lounge-type seats. After a ten-minute ride we arrived at our houseboat. From the outside it didn't look too impressive - a little rickety on the gangplanks and slightly in need of a coat of paint. However, this was misleading as we found out when we entered.

From the front porch we entered a tastefully furnished living room with 2 easy chairs, a chesterfield[30], another couch, a writing desk, coffee table and end tables, etc. all beautifully hand-carved in Kashmir walnut.

From the living room we entered an equally nice dining room with a circular walnut dining room suite, buffet, side-board, etc. Then down a side corridor to the first bedroom with an attached bathroom with toilet, sink, bath-tub and shower (hot and cold running water). Then on to the second double bedroom with its own attached bathroom. The houseboat was at least 40 feet long and 10-12 feet wide. It is moored beside a little peninsula of land with its own little garden, umbrella and deck chairs, etc.

Dal Lake reminds us of Pigeon Lake in Peterborough. It is a shallow, weedy lake with few places where you can't see the weeds growing on the bottom. Almost all the edge would be marshy except that one whole side is cut off by a highway-causeway. The houseboats vary from fairly simple to much more elaborate than ours even. With the houseboat comes a complete "crew" to act as cook, housekeeper, personal guide, etc.

As soon as we had our bags inside, our cook – a good-looking Kashmiri man about 35-40 years old with a typical Persian lamb Kashmiri skull cap brought us tea and freshly made donuts for the "babas" (Hindi for children or babies). After a little sight-seeing ride around the lake we sat down for a dinner of soup, lamb spare ribs, mashed potatoes, small cabbages and a dessert of mixed fruit – cherries and pears. We ate well in spite of earlier snacking on Kashmir walnuts and cherries – our first since we came to India.

We retired early after a long but satisfying day.


June 3rd

We awoke and had a leisurely breakfast of eggs, toast, cereal, etc. around 9:00 a.m. Then with our guide, Mohammad (the owner of our houseboat) went back to our car by shikara and went into town to the tourist bureau to check on our other reservations for Kashmir. We found that we had definite reservations for tourist huts in Pahalgam but no confirmed reservations for Gulmarg or any other place after June 11th.

Then our guide took us shopping in the older part of the city. We learned several things:

1. Many of the prices are not as cheap as Delhi for the same things.
2. Wood-carvings and furniture are an excellent buy.
3. If you go to buy expensive items, don't take your house-boat guide because he gets a "cut" of the profits and that makes it difficult to bargain down to a really good price.

We just priced things and bought a couple of small souvenirs – an embroidered purse for Linda. Then we drove back to the dock and took

---

30 The Canadian term used at the time for a couch or sofa.

the shikara home. Since it was only around 11:30 we decided to go swimming until lunch so we got in the shikara again and went half a mile down the lake to the swimming boats. There, moored in reasonably weed-free water – there are 4 boats which provide diving boards, inner tubes, refreshments and facilities for water skiing and surf-board riding. We just used the swimming facilities – water skiing was very expensive – 2 rupees per minute. Then we returned to lunch.

The afternoon was a time for play and exploring for the children and afternoon sleep for Bill. Before supper we again went out in the shikara and rented a motor boat (in-board car engine powered) for an hour and did some exploring up the lake. Jeff and David both had a chance to drive it. We had a driver-mechanic along too because the motor was rather temperamental. We returned for a delicious supper and spent a quiet, restful evening around the houseboat.

June 4th
After breakfast we decided to take a ride up to Gulmarg by car to see if we could get all our reservations straightened out. The drive is an interesting one. After the first 15 miles it is all up hill. During the next hour we climbed from less than 6,000 feet to 9,000 feet above sea-level. Ahead of us for the last few miles are real snow-capped mountain peaks and beside the road runs a sparkling ice-cold mountain stream. We arrived in Gulmarg and found that cars are not allowed in the actual meadow that houses the tourist huts, hotel, etc. To get to the Highlands Park Hotel to check on reservations we were told we would have to walk about 2/3's of a mile or ride ponies. Since Linda had been sick in the car and wasn't feeling too well and since Margaret was wearing a dress, we looked around for other possibilities and found that we could telephone the hotel from the nearby post office telephone office. A short telephone call confirmed our reservations and after stopping for a Coke – they're really gassy at 9,000 feet! – we got back in the car and started our down-hill ride home. We stopped part way down the mountain for a picnic lunch. Then we stopped at the bottom again to put our feet in the mountain stream. We returned to Srinigar around 4:00 p.m. and shopped until about 5:00 p.m. All the kids bought carved model houseboats. Margaret ordered some clothes for herself and Linda. We decided that we should buy some furniture while we're here but haven't ordered it yet.

The rest of the day was spent back at the houseboat with the children playing with their carved houseboats (which promptly turned over in the water because they were all top-heavy) and catching minnows at the edge of the water.

SOME GENERAL COMMENTS AFTER 3 DAYS HERE:
The People:
Kashmiri people are handsome, hardworking people. We've seen many good-looking girls. There seem to be very few idle people. There is an unbelievably large amount of farming going on all around here – particularly rice but also vegetables, fruits, flowers, etc.

The contrast between these active people and the slow-moving Rajasthanis is very likely a climatic difference. In Srinigar the lake freezes over in the winter. In Rajasthan it is almost always warm.

## The City

The city of Srinigar is a tourist trap. There are handicraft stores with names like "Subhanna, the Worst" and grocery stores called "Cheap John". Shikaras continually ply the lake trying to sell you pop, candy, flowers, jewellery, furs, paintings, etc. etc. Ordinary items are very expensive. Pop is four times the price of Rawat Bhata. Candy bars are twice the cost. Of course, when you realize that everything brought in must come by truck along the same roads we took you can see that transportation costs must be high. The tourist section of the city is well-planned, well-spaced and quite pleasant. The old city is much like Kota - crowded, smelly with people living in poor conditions in small houses or old beat-up houseboats on the river.

## Dal Lake

The lake is not really beautiful but its surroundings tend to make it seem so. It is very weedy and shallow and polluted - as far as we can tell all the houseboat toilets empty into the lake and there are hundreds!

The lake has many disadvantages but it also has mountains towering over it on three sides providing some really breathtaking scenery. There is no unpleasant smell from the lake. It seems very old-fashioned with its houseboats and shikaras. There are only about 10 power boats available on the whole lake and you seldom hear any of these so the overall impression is one of peace and tranquility - a very restful place to spend a holiday.

June 5th
After breakfast went by shikara to the car and visited the remains of the Moghul Gardens overlooking Dal Lake. Although they are still planted with lots of flowers, they gave us just a hint of the opulent

life of the Indian Moghul emperors. After a bit more browsing through the shops (Ahmed Joo's Handicrafts?) we returned home for a delicious Indian lunch – curried lamb, walnut & onion curd, dal (cooked lentils), curried peas, rice, another ground meat curry and caramel custard for dessert. After a short afternoon nap (1½ hrs?) we went by shikara to rent two pedal boats and go swimming. We returned and spent the rest of the afternoon sitting in front of the houseboat reading and half-seriously bartering with half a dozen tradesman that kept appearing with furs, jewellery, etc. etc.

Tomorrow we leave for Pahalgam – trekking and trout fishing from a tourist hut in the mountains. By the way – cost of the houseboat with all meals, services, etc. is about $16 per day. Not bad, eh?

This letter will be continued in a week or so. In the mean time, don't forget to write us. We expect a pile of letters when we return to Township.

Love to all – hope you're having a good summer,
Bill, Marg, Jeff, Linda & David.

Introduction:

This letter is being written in rather unusual circumstances so I thought I would mention those before going back over the last portion of our holiday. It is Friday, June 19th (we think!). I am typing this letter at the table of our Volkswagen Van. It is about 4:30 p.m. and as I look out the window I can see mountains on all sides – many with snow on top, about a million sheep grazing in the fields across the pony track from our van and Jeff, Linda and David running around enjoying the innocent fun of throwing rocks at the sheep, cows, horses, etc. that come into our camp. Margaret is sitting in the van just resting as usual.

June 6th

Left our Srinigar houseboat and drove to Pahalgam. It is about a two-hour drive with the last hour up into the mountains again. Pahalgam is 7,000 ft. above sea level. It is a small town that reminds you of a typical tourist town in Canada. Lots of shops selling food, camping supplies (you can rent any kind of camping gear), local handicrafts – wood carving, embroidery work, jewellery, papier mache work, etc. and other tourist type goodies like pocket books, popcorn, snacks, etc.

We arrived at the tourist office around lunch time. After a wait of about 15 minutes we were told that they had no record of our request for a tourist hut. However, upon seeing the letter which we had confirming our reservations they found that a hut was available.

The "hut" was a very attractive wooden cottage of a very good size by Canadian standards. The interior was a little disappointing but very adequate with two bedrooms with adjoining bathrooms – one Indian and one our style, a large dining room area and an adjoining cabin where the servants could live and prepare the food. Unfortunately we didn't have any of our servants with us so we did not use this at all. We rented a two-burner propane stove to cook on.

The cottage had cold running water with sinks and shower facilities (if you can stand the freezing cold water!)

We spent part of the first day just unpacking and getting settled. When we inquired about a fishing license I was told that they were only available from the Dept. of Fisheries in Srinigar – after just coming from there and being told twice by our houseboat owner that you could get licenses in Pahalgam! Very disappointing but the chowdikar (watchman) for our hut told us that it might be possible to get one anyway. We told him to see what he could do.

June 7th

We went for our first pony ride up into the mountains. It was just a two-hour ride up to a high meadow at about 8,000 ft. I guess. It was pretty and the ponies (really small horses) followed narrow mountain trails that sometimes went right along ledges and through narrow forested sections. It was nice to feel cool air and see so many big trees – a real change from Rajasthan where trees with trunks bigger than a foot are very unusual.

We all enjoyed the riding although each pony had its own guide so you didn't have too much chance of telling it where to go. Since the mountain trail had to be picked pretty carefully I guess the guides are a good idea – particularly your first time out.

After our first ride we came home and rested. We had lunch and spent the rest of the day exploring the town and just resting up.

As you can imagine, our van makes quite an impression up here. Almost everywhere we stop we end up with a small crowd of people peering in the windows. Imported cars are quite rare and a fully outfitted van like ours really causes a sensation.

June 8th

Had our second and most ambitious pony ride to Aru – a distance of 7 miles. This time the ride followed a decent road which went up the river valley from Pahalgam. Lots of gorgeous scenery along the way with snow-fed rushing river in the valley below and snow-capped mountain peaks above. The ride ended at a small village in a high meadow. As well as houses – houses here are often built on the side of a hill out of wood with sod roofs – there was a tourist bungalow for those that wanted to go on up to the glacier – a round trip that takes 3 days from Pahalgam.

After a rest of about an hour, we returned by the same route and arrived home sunburned, tired and sore – not footsore! We decided almost 15 miles on horses was a little too much for us. But it was a very enjoyable trip. Lots of slides to show when we get home. The kids are getting to be pretty good riders. This time we had just two guides for the five horses.

We had supper and another trip into town just browsing through shops, buying books, pricing handicrafts, etc.

June 9th

This was the day of Bill's unfortunate fishing experience! At around 9:00 a.m. the chowdikar and two rather scruffy looking "game wardens?" arrived at our door to say that I could get a fishing license for the day for 18 rupees. I gave the chowdikar 20 rupees and told him to get me the license. About an hour later they returned to say they could issue the license if I would come down to the office. So, I got in the car and drove the two officials back to their office just beyond the town. The office was a one room hut which was used for business, cooking and sleeping. They asked me the information and began to fill in the form. I asked if there were any special rules or regulations I should know. They said that the trout "beat" that I had allowed only fly fishing. I told them that I didn't have any flies at all – just spoons, spinners, etc. They said well that was all right, they would take care of that for me. They issued the license and I said I would go home and get my family and we would all go down to the beat. They advised me to pick them up on the way and they would show me its location.

When we arrived at the beat I got out my tackle box and they both had a good look at it shaking their heads ruefully. Only flies can be used on this beat! After a few minutes checking through the box and discussion in Hindi (or Urdu) the warden chose a small spinner and made it clear that although it was against the regulations, they would let me use it implying that I would probably want to make it worth their while to overlook this rule. So, with this small spinner – one of the most unattractive lures in my tackle box – they suggested that I cast into the rapids below the bridge where we were parked. It was obvious after two casts that both the lure and location were unsuitable. I suggested this and said I didn't want to break the regulations anyway.

The warden said that the shikar (guide) for the beat would be along pretty soon and would bring some flies and spoons to use. Just about then it started to rain and we waited in the rain for about 20 minutes. Then I gave up and decided to go home. On the way back in the car we met the shikar with a little tin box containing one scraggly fly and several spoons. He offered to sell them to me. I bought the fly for 2 rupees but decided that fishing was out of the question with so many people to be paid off so I gave up and decided to give up on fishing in Pahalgam. Too much graft – at least the way I tried it.

In the afternoon we took a car ride down the valley of the Lidder river. Kashmir has impressed us with its hard-working people and fertile farm land. The river we followed had been diverted in countless places down the valley to provide irrigation for fields. Rice is a very common crop. We have seen acres and acres of rice paddies planted in the Japanese method with flooded fields. Also we found Kashmiri people attractive, reasonably well-dressed with many really good-looking children. Some of the people are very light-skinned. If you dressed some of the children in our children's clothing they could pass for Canadians easily.

Another enjoyable aspect of Kashmir was the fruit available here. We bought fresh cherries, apricots, peaches, etc. and fresh vegetables which were better than any we had had since we left Canada.

June 10th

Took a short pony ride up the mountain opposite our side of town to "Big Chicargah". The ride followed a narrow mountain path up to a clear glacier-fed stream. The children looked really professional on the ponies now. We took a roll of movie film on the way up so you'll get some idea of what it was like.

In the late afternoon we went up to a camp site to visit 3 ladies from Uttar Pradesh. They had seen our van on the way in and one of the ladies was very interested in buying a van just like ours and driving it back across Europe from India. All three worked in an interdenominational medical hospital which worked in the Indian villages in Uttar Pradesh (an Indian state about 200 miles from Rajasthan). We had an interesting visit comparing notes on India, etc. One of the doctors came from Toronto. One of them had been in India for 9 years, one 7 years and one for 4 years. The one that had been here for 7 years is going home next summer for a furlough (probably a year).

We had an interesting visit and left feeling our puny two-year stay was nothing in comparison. There are no other Canadians within 100 miles of their hospital so you can imagine how much harder their life is than ours.

June 11th

Went on a very lucky car tour. We decided to follow a road we had discovered one night close to dark. According to the signs, it goes to Chandiwarah but we stopped on our first attempt when we got to a sign saying "Jeepable Road Beyond This Point". It turned out that the road was very passable and we spent about an hour and a half climbing a steep, twisting road up the mountain. We arrived at the little town of Chandiwarah which is only there to serve tourists. Every store is a tent where they serve tea, juice, and some simple Indian foods, cookies, etc. at fairly expensive prices. Just past Chandiwarah – about 300 yards – there is a permanent ice bridge crossing the river and so we all walked on snow and ice in the middle of June after not seeing any all winter.

We also had tea (Indian recipe is loaded with milk and sugar), the kids had juice and we had a package of cookies. Then we drove back down the mountain in the rain. I think there were only two cars who went to Chandiwarah that day. Everyone else walked up or went by pony. You can guess how many people we had asking for a lift but we were hard-hearted and already had a fairly heavily-loaded car for the trip so we ignored their requests in true white-sahib fashion.

June 12th

We packed up our tourist hut and moved half a mile down the road to the Nataraj Hotel. We decided that we needed a hotel to get cleaned up in and to get some variety in our meals again. We moved into a two-bedroom hotel room on the second floor overlooking the grounds and settled in for a nice quiet day with some walking and some quite decent hotel meals and a hot bath!

June 13th

Spent the day doing more exploring by car and on foot and eating hotel meals. It was the best hotel in Pahalgam but it was pretty low by Canadian standards. The dining room made you think you were eating in a church basement - but the rooms were comfortable and the food decent.

June 14th

Left Pahalgam for Sonamarg by way of Srinigar. For the second time we just made it back to the main highway in time for the gas station. There is no gas station in Pahalgam. You have to drive 40 miles from there before you can get gas but we made it. Earlier in the week we had to make the 80 mile round trip just to fill the tank - some fun!

We arrived in Srinigar around 12:30 and spent some time looking in wood stores and comparing prices for furniture. It looks like we could get a beautiful hand-carved dining room suite made to our specifications for well under $200. We haven't ordered it yet but we're thinking about it!

After checking with the tourist bureau Bill got a proper trout fishing license for a beat near Sonamarg and then we went to pick up a small tent and some camping supplies. We rented an 8x8 tent, two camp chairs and a ground sheet from a camping outfitter in Srinigar. It took about an hour and a half to get it but we did. Then we bought some food and left around 3:30 p.m. for Sonamarg - another 85 miles.

Once again the drive was beautiful with the last 20 miles threading its way through a river valley between the mountains. Sonamarg is a very small town! There are about 8 stores and about 12 houses. The stores really serve the tourist buses and taxis that arrive every day.

The tourist bureau said we could camp anywhere we wanted so we found a nice spot at the foot of the mountain about half a mile from the town and set up camp. The tent was meant for storing all the junk we carry in the car. We soon found that it provided a little privacy for a bathroom as well. We used our portable toilet for the first time and found it quite satisfactory. After a supper cooked on an open fire we set up the van and made the beds and spent our first night in our camping van. It was quite comfortable and we all slept quite well.

June 15th
Had a quiet day exploring the town, watching a thousand army trucks
pass through – the army is crawling all over Kashmir protecting its
borders from Pakistan invaders – and generally enjoying the scenery.

   After some rain in the early afternoon, we decided to go for a
walk. We had been told there was a glacier 4 or 5 miles away and
headed in that general direction. Although we hadn't intended to walk
too far we kept going and going and actually got all the way to the
glacier – actually it is a number of glaciers with snow-capped
mountain peaks and sides all up the valley. After stopping at the
inevitable tourist tent for tea, Jeff, David and Bill decided to walk
up to the lowest ice – another half-mile climb from the tourist stop.
Before we were half-way there it started to rain. We got up there but
arrived back soaking wet and very cold. By now it was really pouring
with rain and we had the problem of how to get back without any
jackets, etc. There was no alternative to walking. All the ponies had
left for the day and there was no road so we waited for a lull in the
storm and started out. The rain varied from pouring to spitting all
the way home and we arrived looking like cold, drowned rats.
Fortunately we could put on the car heater – a special gas-burning
one in our camping van - and we were soon dry again with no one
suffering any ill effects.

June 16th
We left in the morning for Bill's trout beat – about 20 miles south
of Sonamarg. With the help of the local shikar, caught 6 trout in
about 3 hours when it started to rain. We came home and had a
delicious trout dinner cooked on an open fire.

   Had rain in the evening for the second night in a row, so we sat
in the van drinking pop, playing cards (piggy was the game!) and
listening to our portable tape recorder. The kids went to bed late
and we went to bed early – all at the same time.

June 17th

More fishing in the morning. Again the fishing was good. Bill caught six more trout in about 3 hours - a little bigger than the day before. The biggest one was about 13 inches long, the smallest around 9 or 10 inches.

Again we ran into gas trouble. We were down to a quarter of a tank of gas. We had stopped at one gas station near the fishing beat and that was for private use only. The man there told us that we could get gas at a town 10 miles farther south toward Srinigar. We drove there and found that we would have to go all the way back to Srinigar. According to the gas gauge, we just made it. We filled the tank and used our trip to buy part of David's birthday present. Then we discovered a pretty decent bakery and bought David a birthday cake. Then we discovered a restaurant that sold infra-red cooked chicken in a basket, soft ice cream and popcorn! Wow! We went in and had a very nice lunch although we had to order three times before we were understood and then part of the order was goofed up.

We left Srinigar to come back to Sonamarg feeling much better about the trip.

June 18th

David's birthday is today! He got his presents first thing in the morning - a pogo stick (the only one in Delhi!), a "computer" book which has a gimmicky method of asking questions and giving the answers using a "magic" pointer which works with a magnet, and a hand-carved Kashmiri knife in a wooden sheath.

David spent most of the morning playing with his presents. Linda got one of those glass birds that drink from a glass continually and we gave Jeffrey part of his present - a Kashmiri knife like David's. They all had fun on the pogo stick.

For lunch we had fried potatoes, trout, stewed tomatoes and birthday cake! Pretty good birthday for the wilds of Sonamarg!

In the afternoon we had a pony ride for about an hour and saw some of the houses in the village of Sonamarg. Most are built of wood - a plentiful material around here. It rained around late afternoon and we came in the van for another game of cards - then cooked hot dogs wrapped in dough on a stick and had onion soup for supper. We had a camp fire for a while, but it was still a bit wet so we all came in and went to bed fairly early.

June 19th

Awoke to a lovely sunny day. Had breakfast and Bill went for a hike with the kids. They walked about a mile up river to a spot where a mountain stream joins the river. There they followed the stream about half-way to the top. It was the closest to mountain climbing they've done - they had to use a rope to get up several places but it was very exciting. The top was too far to go but the climb was fun and they had a nice cold drink of water from the mountain stream. Lots of cold, clear water around here.

After lunch, we decided to take a drive north of Pahalgam. We went three miles when we were stopped at an army check post and told that we couldn't go any further. We came back and drove down to a spot on the river where we could wash the car. Bill washed while the kids made dams and rivers and Marg sat. We returned with a freshly washed and waxed car, the cleanest in Sonamarg (maybe the only after the tourist cars leave!) Had a supper of corned mutton (?) made into a stew. Then Bill and the kids had an exciting trip in to the town for eggs, cookies and some candies.

Tomorrow we leave for Gulmarg where we'll stay at the Highlands Park Hotel. Oh for a good bath after camping for 6 days!

That's all for now. Keep writing. We look forward to those letters!

Marg, Bill, Jeff, Linda and David (who is 7).

# Kashmir Diary – Part III (final)

This letter is being written at our dining room table in township. Our trip is complete, so here's the story from leaving Sonamarg.

June 20th

Packed up our camping equipment and left for Srinigar to return our rented tent. As we came down through the mountains we had one last look at the rushing, glacier-fed rivers and miles of rice paddies that are so important to this area.

We arrived in Srinigar for lunch at our favourite Srinigar restaurant where we ordered Chicken Kiev. After a long wait (35 minutes?) it arrived – tender pieces of chicken wrapped in a single brown batter with mashed potato and other accessories all shaped together in the form of a hen! It was really nice-looking and delicious too.

In the afternoon we left for the next part of our holiday – 5 days at the Highlands Park Hotel in Gulmarg. Gulmarg is a meadow nine thousand feet up on the side of a mountain. The road there is strange – you think you are travelling on the level but actually you are continually climbing as you can tell from the trouble your car has accelerating and getting into fourth gear (if it's a Volkswagen). The final section of the road climbs about two thousand feet through lovely evergreen woodlands with some beautiful scenery.

We arrived in the parking lot at the edge of Gulmarg and immediately began attempting to get our car to the hotel. According to regulations you are supposed to park there and walk 3/4's of a mile to the hotel. This is particularly undesirable because you have to hire porters for your luggage for the trip too. We were met at the lot by a hotel attendant and told that it usually wasn't possible to get our car past the barrier where the guard was on duty but after about 10 minutes of fooling around they finally agreed to let us go up to the hotel by an alternate route which saved quite a bit of time and expense - after all they cost 2 rupees each for the trip! (30¢).

The hotel is laid out in separate cabins and in units containing 3 or 4 cabins each. We were given two nice adjoining units with a large bedroom and bathroom in each including a small wood stove. We spent the rest of the day unpacking, exploring and having a nice hot bath again.

June 21st

In the morning we went on our first pony trek to Killanmarg – a meadow about 2,000 feet higher than Gulmarg which overlooks it. The ponies were big and healthy and the trip through more evergreen forest was most enjoyable. It took all morning and we found that we are becoming very seasoned riders.

During the afternoon we took a walk and had a restful...

*Interesting Note: At this point I was interrupted by the wife of the cook next door who, after some translating from her husband, said she saw a snake. I got out the car spotlight and checked our neighbour's front lawn and discovered a two-foot Bamboo Pit Viper (poisonous). Just then, our next-door neighbour arrived himself and, with the help of his six-foot long bamboo "snake axe", killed it before it even knew what had happened.*

*In spite of the fact that it was in three pieces Ramu, the cook, insisted that he crush the head along with the Hindu belief that the spirit of the snake will haunt you if you don't destroy the head. Now back to the newsletter...*

...time generally doing some reading, etc. The meals here were excellent with a choice of Indian or Western food.

June 22nd
Jeffrey's birthday. He got a motorized model of a Japanese battleship to build, a "computer book" something like David's but harder, two Hardy Boys books and a Kashmiri knife.

In the morning I (Bill) went out for a game of golf. There is a lovely golf course there – 18 holes plus club house, practice field, putting green, etc. I did some practising for half an hour and then played twelve holes of golf with one of the teaching pros.

The course is in lovely shape. All the fairways are kept cut by a large flock of sheep which are herded from section to section, usually in the late afternoon. I played badly since I hadn't touched a club for a year, but found the game enjoyable.

In the afternoon we had some rain and the weather was quite cool. We actually needed a fire in our stove! What a nice change from township.

At lunch time Jeff had a special birthday cake in the dining room where we all sang "Happy Birthday". His main comment was "I wish we'd had it in our room!" with an embarrassed grin.

June 23rd
Woke up to rain. It rained almost all day. The kids played around – mostly inside reading comic books. Jeff started work on his model boat. Quite a cool, uncomfortable, wet day. Nothing very exciting happened.

June 24th
Went on a pony trek in the morning to a meadow at 13,000 feet. It was cloudy and we had a picnic lunch on the meadow almost completely surrounded by clouds. The track was rather muddy from the previous day's rain so it was a little treacherous for the ponies but they were pretty sure-footed. Several times we forded deep streams on pony-back. Hope we get good pictures! A very enjoyable trip – our most expensive, too. For the approximate 5-hour trip with 4 pony-wallahs and five horses, the total cost including a generous tip was about $6.00

In the afternoon I met the pro and played 18 holes of golf. I played much better this time – in fact I generally out-drove the pro.

June 25th
Left Gulmarg after a final pony trip across the meadow back to the car lot. Got stuck for a small parking fee in their crummy, muddy lot and was rather mad since I didn't want to leave my car there anyway.

Drove back to Srinigar and got a suite at the Oberoi Palace Hotel. Bill wasn't feeling too well so he had a rest while Marg and the children enjoyed the buffet lunch in the main dining room. Since they were fairly early and there were very few others in there, the band played "Canadian Sunset" and children's songs all the time they were there.

After lunch we went to our favourite wood carving shop and went on a tour of wood-carving factories in old Srinigar. We threaded our way through streets as narrow as any in Kota and visited two "factories" and a show-room. In one, we saw the progress on the coffee table and end tables we had ordered. In two others we saw dining room suites they are building. We are interested in a dining room suite and the man has promised to send us plans according to the specifications we have given plus price. It looks like a good, hand-carved dining room suite here costs about the same as a decent chrome and arborite one in Canada, so we'll see. The suites we saw partially done were just beautiful.

Bought more junk as gifts and souvenirs and went back to the hotel. Then we got on a shikara and visited two other families from township who were staying on houseboats. Later in the evening they stopped into the hotel for a visit and a drink.

June 26th
Left Srinigar and drive back through the mountains to Jammu – an
exhausting day's drive but beautiful scenery. Arrived in Jammu around
6:00 p.m. and reserved two air-conditioned tourist rooms just as we
did on the way up. Found a decent restaurant for some dinner and
bought some books and went to bed.

June 27th
Drove from Jammu to Simla[31]. Simla is a hill station in Himachal
Pradesh (an Indian state) also in the Himalayas (actually it's only
350 kilometres from Tibet). This was our longest day's drive. It was
straight, fairly fast highway driving until around 5:00 p.m. There
was 70 miles of twisting, turning mountain driving where 20 m.p.h.
was a good average. We arrived exhausted at 8:30 p.m. to Oberoi
Clark's Hotel in Simla to found that our telegrammed request for
reservations from Srinigar had not been received. Fortunately rooms
were available and we got a suite. Rates here were the best ever. It
cost about $12.00 per day total for the five of us to stay at the
hotel – including <u>all meals</u>.

June 28th
Explored Simla on foot. Simla is a fair-sized city built right on the
side of a mountain. Each house is almost on top of the one below it.
The hotels, stores and roads are all just cut into the side of a
hill. It is very unreal.
     The day was cloudy – raining at times – and the whole place has
the unreal quality of being back in time about thirty years. Lots of
people move around – all carrying umbrellas and all walking. The
stores are very nice with soft ice cream and pop and popcorn all for

---

31  Now known as Shimla.

sale at very reasonable prices. A Coke costs 30¢ (luke warm) in Kashmir. Ice cold Cokes are 7 or 8¢ here. There are all sorts of souvenir stalls selling toys, canes, brass and copper work, clothing, materials, books, etc., etc.

We had an enjoyable day walking around, buying junk and just exploring. We decided Simla would be a good place for a fairly quiet and inexpensive holiday.

Simla is serviced by quite decent roads plus a narrow gauge (30-inch) railway that was built back in 1903 by the British at a cost of millions of rupees. You can imagine building 70 miles of railway through the beginnings of the Himalayas - there are over 100 tunnels in that stretch. Trains bring goods and tourists up on a five-hour run from the town at the beginning of the mountains.

June 29th
Left Simla and drove to Delhi. Arrived around 6:00 p.m. and checked in at the Imperial Hotel into a family suite. Had dinner and went to bed. It's a long drive and not too interesting when you've seen it all before. Delhi is hot as usual and the pool at the Imperial isn't open.

June 30th
Shopped and did some sight-seeing in Delhi. Went over to Claridges to have dinner with the C--'s who are staying there. The kids enjoyed visiting with them.

July 1st
Spent part of the day shopping and window-shopping. Left the kids at the apartment of a Canadian embassy member and went to the Canadian Embassy cocktail party for Canada's birthday. We spent from 6:30 to 8:00 p.m. drinking cocktails, snacking and generally being overwhelmed by the huge crowd of about 150 Canadians including about half of the adults in township. Went back to the Imperial with friends from township and had a nice dinner after putting the kids to bed. The kids had "imported" Canadian pizza for their supper at the apartment.

July 2nd
Bill played golf at the Delhi Golf Club with three other men from township. It's a lovely course - beautifully kept and no one on it on a Friday at least. Shot a 91.

Shopped and did some sight-seeing in the afternoon. In the evening we joined 10 other township couples on the top floor restaurant of the Oberoi Intercontinental Hotel for dinner. The food was good but slow with so many of us ordering at the same time. There was a live dance band that was very good plus a singer wearing "hot pants".

Good restaurants are inexpensive by Canadian standards. Our bill for two was just over $6.00 after ordering one of the most expensive items on the menu – Chateaubriand steak for two.

July 3rd
More time shopping and sight-seeing. Bill spent part of the afternoon shopping for a multi-media kit on India to take back for use in Etobicoke schools. The rest of the family bought clothes and other things you can't buy in township.

Again the kids were left with a baby-sitter and we went out to a dinner party at the home of a Canadian Embassy member, Miss N-- F--. The dinner party was for R.A.P.P. Township people with a couple of other guests included. It was lovely and we left around 11:30 to return to the Imperial restaurant for coffee with 3 other R.A.P.P. couples. This ended when the power went off and we all used candles to get back to our rooms where the power conveniently came back on.

July 4th
Left Delhi for Township. Drove all day and arrived around 7:00 p.m. after 36 days away from home – a pretty long holiday.

Some General Observations:
The vacation spots of northern India are lovely but many of them look a little like ghost towns because of the large number of tourist huts, cottages, etc. which are entirely deserted. The British made excellent use of these areas in the summer months. Not nearly as many Indians can afford to do so and so far, India hasn't been able to encourage nearly enough foreign tourist trade. The result is too much accommodation for too few people and much of it in a state of partial or complete ruin.

The Car:
The car ran beautifully on the trip. I never even changed a tire. Two of the four vans in township have had trouble with steering dampers resulting in a lot of shimmying but so far no trouble with ours[32]. I do have a slow leak in a front tire which I'll have to check and the motor has a rather strange low-pitched roaring sound it didn't have before, but performance-wise no trouble yet. We particularly enjoyed it for camping. That will be fun in Canada[33].

The Weather:
The weather was much like Canadian summer weather during our trip with quite a bit of rain and cool nights. We could have stayed longer, but monsoon has begun and some of the roads home would become impassable pretty soon. Rajasthan is hot and sticky. It has already begun to get green with a few days of rain.

---

32  We later had the steering damper on our van fail.
33  We did use the van in Canada for several years, including a number of camping trips.

## The House:

The house survived for the month quite well. When we checked the upstairs bathroom we found two large bugs and a scorpion in the bath tub. Lots of bugs around. The crickets have started again. The garden looks very nice. Our cook is back on the job but we are getting a new sweeper tomorrow.

## Other News:

We have now been presented with a real problem. Thanks to the enthusiasm of the local community for the present mode of operation of the school, we have been asked by A.E.C.L. to consider staying for a third year. The offer includes a two-month home leave next summer (which is really a free trip around the world for five) plus the usual guarantees of a contract with Etobicoke when we return. We are considering the problem and won't decide until September or October at the earliest.

Well that's all for now. Love from, Bill, Marg, Jeff, Linda and David.

This letter is written from our dining room table as usual again. No more holiday trips since our last ones. The house looks rather different from a month ago. The colours on the walls have changed somewhat. They are gray and spotted. What is the gray colour? It is moss, mould and mildew. What caused it? Monsoon has arrived!

## The Weather

Out of the last seven days, it has rained steadily for at least six of them and the other day only managed sunlight for a few hours. Roads are muddy and flooded out in places. The ground is squishy. All the houses (and school) are leaking. There is a pail on the floor about five feet from me catching drips from the ceiling. The ceiling has a ring of dampness around it. The den, children's bedroom, living room, etc. all have at least one wall covered with monsoon mould.

Last Friday Bill drove to Kota for shopping for school supplies. After supper he drove in again to take neighbours to the railroad station. There are about thirty places where water flows on the road (Jeff counted them!). Just outside Kota, there was a place where the road was flooded across for about fifty feet in length with water that got up to 12-18 inches deep. But the car plowed through. We are finishing up a roll of movie film with pictures of monsoon. We'll send it along soon.

In the mean time, monsoon continues with umbrellas inside and out!

## Our New Pet

Today we got a new pet. It is a six-week-old grey and white kitten. One of a litter born at a neighbour's house. The mother is a domestic cat and the father was one of the small wild-cats that roam our community at night. We hope this one will be like its mother. We have called it "Mandu". Actually its full name is "Cat Mandu" – named after the city of Katmandu in Nepal which overlooks Mount Everest. Right now it is curled up asleep beside Margaret on the chesterfield. The kids think it is great and have "played" with the poor thing ever since we got it. It should sleep well tonight – if it doesn't miss its mother and brothers and sisters too much! If it does cause a lot of trouble or nuisance during the night – well, it's Margaret's cat so she'll have to look after it! He is a male and looks very much like Muffy[34].

## A Disappointment

In Delhi Bill got a new windshield for his Rajdoot motorcycle. Last week, one day, he swung his leg over the saddle, pushed it forward off the kick-stand and smash! His leg caught on one of the boy's bicycles and there was nothing to support the motorcycle. It

---

34  Our cat back in Canada, being taken care of by our grandparents when we were in India.

fell against the garage wall breaking both the rear-view mirror and the new windshield. So - after about a week of use the windshield was removed, He now has a letter to Delhi requesting a replacement plastic windshield. So far there has been no answer. So once again, you can tell the motorcycle driver in the crowd - by the bugs in his teeth!

## Shopping in Kota

Just a word to remind you how lucky you are to live in an area where English is easily understood. Last week in Kota Bill had to buy several unusual things such as some solder and a hack saw. It is not easy to go into a hardware store where no-one speaks English and get a hack saw. However, with some pointing and action he got one. It took three stores to get the solder before he finally came across someone who recognized the word even though it is the same in India.

Even with English-speaking store-keepers communication can be a problem. Margaret went into a shoe store to buy Linda some new rubber boots. They didn't know what rubber boots were. Then it dawned on them - Oh, you mean gum boots! In school supplies we translate thumb tacks as drawing pins, glue as gum and workbooks as copy books. At least we'll have lots of new words in our vocabulary when we return.

## Summer School

Last week, Margaret and another former teacher ran a one-week summer vacation school from 9:30 a.m. to 12:00 noon each day. They used the theme of Canada and a programme based on a Canadian Church summer school programme for any children in the community. The bored kids in township really enjoyed it and of course the mothers were all pleased to get their kids out of the way for the morning each day.

It was a real success and got the kids in training a bit for school next week without giving them too much work. They did crafts, games, had stories and a slide presentation about Canada and many other things. On Friday they ended up with a party which was enjoyed by all.

## Plans for School

School starts again next Monday. There is still lots of preparation to be done. There won't be too many changes this year, but because of the numbers Bill will have grades 4, 5, 6, 7 and 8. That means that both Linda and Jeffrey will be in his class. Lucky kids! Poor David will still be in Mrs. W--'s class. We have four in the Kindergarten class with our Indian Kindergarten teacher, Mrs. R--. We're still waiting for a big load of supplies from Canada which should have been here ages ago but has been held up because the customs people can't get around to issuing an import license. Luckily we can get along without the new supplies for the first few weeks.

## One Year In India

Last Sunday we celebrated exactly one year in R.A.P.P. Township with a dinner party at our house for five couples. They arrived between 8:00 and 8:30 p.m. After one or two drinks we had dinner at nine - sweet & sour balled chicken and pork, steamed rice, Chinese beef, fried prawns (shrimp) salad, three kinds of bread, grapefruit juice with peach shortcake, butter tarts and brownies for dessert and coffee. After dinner (around 10:00 p.m.) you'll never guess what we did! We played some party games! Of course, Bill didn't want to, but Margaret forced him into it again. The games lasted until after 11:00 and the party broke up around 12:00 a.m. Everyone seemed to have a good time. Just in case you are pitying Margaret, she didn't have to do any of the menial preparations although she did exhaust herself supervising the cook. Bill also hired an additional man to come in and serve drinks so he wouldn't have to get up all the time and do it himself - so exhausting, you know! Anyway, we celebrated the dubious honour of having spent a year in R.A.P.P. Township just as if it were a big event.

## Laugh-In '72

Bill and another township comedian are already madly at work writing scripts and skit ideas for next year's big Laugh-In in township. It will be held this December. Preliminary script outlines for the two big spectaculars are already prepared and there are lots of skits partly planned too. It should be bigger and better and funnier than ever! Don't be surprised if you're asked to get some crazy item or record and ship it over here before then.

## Films

We got our first Kashmir slides back yesterday. They turned out very well but there are still two boxes to be returned. We expect them any day now. Have you seen our films yet? How did they turn out? Do you have any questions about them? There must be quite a stack of movies back there now. There's still half a roll of movie film taken in Gulmarg in the camera but we're finishing it with monsoon pictures so that will be along soon.

By the way, how about some pictures from you? Is there anybody back there with pictures of pets, children, new houses or summer vacation fun that can afford to send a few pictures over to their poor Indian relatives? Also, a special word to you movie camera owners. We have a projector over here going to waste. How about a roll of movie film once in a while? Just remember to send it air mail registered.

Well, that's all for now. Write soon. Love from all,

Bill, Marg, Jeff, Linda and David.

## Poor Margaret!

As I (Bill) sit here typing this newsletter, Margaret is slaving in the kitchen! That's right! She's in there right now doing dishes! Of course its a little awkward because she couldn't remember whether you put them in the soapy water before or after you wipe them with the dish towel, but it's all coming back to her. You see, today we lost our second cook since the beginning of our stay in India. He decided to leave partly because he is getting close to retirement age and would like to get back to his wife and family in Bombay. It is also because Margaret didn't approve of his rather heavy drinking habit. He was always sober during the day but he drank pretty heavily in the evening and it threatened to become a problem so she gave him an alternative of cutting down on the drinking and parties or quitting. He thought about it and decided to leave. He was a pretty good fellow and we gave him a good letter of reference.

So that leaves Margaret in the kitchen – temporarily at least. She's just about figured out how to use the oven and tomorrow she's trying something on the top burners of the stove. Actually, of course, it isn't that bad. She's been keeping in practice by burning the toast at breakfast herself every morning! You can be sure that by the next letter we will have hired our third cook. Shall we hire one for you too? [Handwritten comment added by Marg: *As you can see by Bill's sweet comments, he hasn't changed at all.*]

## Monsoon Weather

Our weather has been nicer again recently. We've had rain regularly but we've had a lot of sunshine too, so things aren't as wet and soggy all over as they were several weeks ago. This is actually a very nice time of year in this part of India. The weather is reasonably cool – low 80's. Everything is growing like mad. It's not too much different than a very wet, humid Canadian summer.

## A Little Visitor

On Saturday night we had a little visitor. We were sitting in our living room chatting with the W——s when suddenly out across the floor walked a brown scorpion about 2½ inches long. He had his tail over his back ready to strike. We assume he came in around a crack in the door which wasn't properly bolted. We didn't give him a very nice welcome. After about three swats with a fly swatter he rolled over and died (poor thing). This one was the brown kind that give a painful but not serious sting so we didn't treat it as a real emergency at the time but he did give us a surprise.

## The Crisis in East Pakistan

A number of people have asked us about the East Pakistan problem and whether it has any effect on us. The simple answer is "no – not so far". Of course news coverage of it has been very intensive in this area since the beginning of the Pakistani conflict. India is obviously strongly on the side of the so-called "Bangladesh Freedom Fighters" and is harbouring the single greatest group of refugees in the history of the world. The East-West Pakistan conflict has resulted in a very tense political situation in which India is insisting that the refugees must be reinstated and the West Pakistanis are continuing with their cruel treatment of any East Pakistanis showing resistance. There are a number of indications that India and Pakistan are on the verge of war again. This week's Times of India Weekly has a large colour article on a comparison of India's and Pakistan's military might – assuring the people that India couldn't help but win. Last week India signed a rather significant treaty agreement with Russia that also heightened tension. (Pakistan considers Red China and the U.S. allies – though this is somewhat embarrassing to the U.S.) This week's Asian issue of Time magazine says that there is a 50% chance of war in the immediate future. It seems unlikely that this will be more than a series of prolonged border conflicts even if it does develop.

The health problems of the refugees (such as the spread of cholera) seems fairly well contained in Eastern India. There has been no definite sign of it in our area although several rumours of it are floating around. We have all had cholera shots and are in good health anyway so it does not represent a threat to us.

Of course the outbreak of a war could be a serious threat. In that case, the Canada-India agreement for the building of the plant would terminate immediately and we would all be sent home. It's even in our contract that in case of evacuation because of the outbreak of war we would be completely compensated for all goods that we have to leave behind.

The next few weeks will probably be very significant. In fact some change for either the better or worse will likely occur before you receive this letter.

Independence Day

Yesterday was India's Independence Day. On August 15th, 1947 India became an independent nation. It is a day for celebration in India – particularly for patriotic speeches, flag-raising ceremonies, etc. The staff and students of our school were invited to the neighbouring Indian school to see a flag-raising ceremony, gymnastic display, hear some speeches by the children and from the guest of honour (the chief project engineer). Our kids sang two songs (about Canada) and were part of the audience for the rest. We got off to a bad start when the buses arranged by the Indian school to pick us up were an hour late so we missed the first 15 minutes of the programme. Another Indian custom on Independence Day is to distribute "sweets" to the children. Each of our pupils received a little plastic bag containing a banana, several kinds of Indian candy, several wrapped hard candies and some crispy fried snack-type stuff something like spiced shoestring potatoes. It was interesting to try some typical

151

Indian sweets. We often see it on sale in Rawat Bhata but when you have no idea what it tastes like you hesitate to buy it.

There are certainly very significant differences between the Indian and Canadian school philosophies. Here there is a strong emphasis on marching, repetition, and speeches with strong emotional appeals rather than logic and standardization. Our students can't march as well but they have more individual initiative and are much more capable of critical thinking. There is certainly more than a hint of military atmosphere in the schools and a very strong military atmosphere in their scouting movement.

Hobby Time!

Well, it's hobby time around the old community. During the last two weeks three of the local men (Bill is one) have been building a slot car racing track. They must have set a new record for production time. In exactly two weeks of spare time (or about 150 man-hours) they built a four-lane 50-foot long slot car track powered by one of the most sophisticated electrical systems you have ever seen (thanks to the other two guys working for Ontario Hydro). The track is built on three 4x8 sheets of chipboard with the slots carefully carved out of the wood. It has one overpass and completely fills an upstairs bedroom of one of the houses. Cars raced on it yesterday for the first time. Of course there is still work to be done building retaining walls, doing landscaping, finishing-up work, etc. but the track is basically complete – the fastest in two ways – high speed track and high-speed construction!

The second thing that has been built in the last two weeks is a go-cart for Jeff and David. Jeff and his dad designed a go-cart frame made out of 5/8 inch wrought iron, took the design over to Rawat Bhata and had it all welded up. It was ready two days later at a cost of just about $3.00 (including materials). We added plywood floorboards and backrest (old packing case wood) and "revolutionary" rope steering system, a brake, a beautifully upholstered seat and back rest (courtesy of Mom) and a rear-view mirror (repaired Rajdoot motorcycle style). Now they have a fastest go-cart in township much to the consternation of the other half-dozen boys (and fathers) who own go-carts. The winners!

More About the School:

A week ago Friday we had a big desk-painting "bee" in my class. All the kids in grades 6, 7, 8 wore their old clothes and they painted their ordinary crummy wood-coloured desks in their choice of bright red, sky blue or grass green (no combinations allowed). With the grade 4's and 5's to help they spent all of Friday afternoon painting and cleaning up. On Monday the desks were quite dry and our classroom has bloomed into colour. Just don't try to go in without your sunglasses!

School supplies from Canada continue to be a problem in our school. We ordered supplies through A.E.C.L. last March and April. They were assembled along with a new 16 m.m. projector for air freighting to India. Then they began the wait for clearance from D.A.E. in Bombay that an import license has been issued for to allow the shipment into the country. D.A.E. got around to applying in June. It was still not issued in the middle of July when A.E.C.L. finally gave up and shipped it without an import license. Now we assume it is in Bombay (probably for a month already at least). So we carry on bravely waiting for our new texts, workbooks, projector (sob!) etc.

Furniture is also a problem. D.A.E. (and in fact all of India) is a bewildering mass of red tape (the English influence?). As early as last February I began ordering new desks, bulletin boards, book shelves, etc. for the school. So far we managed to get just a few shelves and some new chairs but no desks. To give you an idea of the problem, I've sent three memos and had one meeting at the plant trying to get two new waste baskets. The closest I've come so far is a promise that I'll get two some time this week. I'm not really too optimistic though. There is a strong tendency in this country to promise anything you want to hear and worry about the consequences later.

The new school addition is coming along slowly. They are just beginning to pour the concrete on the roof of one of the largest classrooms. First they build the plywood and bamboo frame. Then they seal the joints with mud. Then the work women carry the basins of cement up a ramp on their head and dump it on the roof. After it has set they knock out all the supports and hope the roof doesn't collapse.

Actually we're a little worried about that right now. The roof was originally designed with two additional dividing walls in it. They were removed when the plans changed. We don't know if any changes were made in the specifications of the roof to allow for the lack of support. Engineers are investigating right now. If it's decided that the roofing is not safe the construction may be held up for months. It's a good thing we've already got reasonably decent classrooms in the mean time.

By the way, I've never written so many memos in my life!

Love
Bill & Marg, Jeff, Linda & David.

Weather:

    Just as I sat down to write this letter a minor hurricane has come up. The wind is shrieking through our driveway and whipping our poor papaya trees all over the place. The rain is coming down in sheets which will undoubtedly start a number of near "rivers" in the roads and low places. Here the ground is so sandy and rocky that any hard rainfall doesn't sink in – it just flows down in rivers and streams which get deeper and faster until they are actually big enough to sweep people away. Of course you have to be silly enough to be walking in or near a known watercourse for it to happen but the rivers do come up here very suddenly. I have heard that a one-hour rain in the right place can flood part of the road to Kota up to three feet deep. I've seen it flooded almost 2 feet deep (and driven through it).

    Actually the weather has been very pleasant lately. The monsoon rains have not been too regular or too heavy – just enough to provide some cooling evaporation. It is just like a hot day in summer in Canada. It's a good thing the weather hasn't been too hot. There are lots of outdoor activities discussed in the letter that follows.

Opening the Dam

    As you probably know, we live within a mile of Rana Pratap Sagar (R.P.S.) Dam which holds back a reservoir of water nearly 20 miles long and several miles wide. It is named after Rana Pratap – a famous Indian warrior of about 200 years ago. During the time we have been here the dam has remained almost completely closed except for the regular amount of water which passes through the turbines to generate electricity. Last week, however, the next dam up river, Ghandi Sagar (sagar means "lake") opened up. It is at the bottom end of a much larger reservoir so when it opened ours began to fill rather quickly. So they broke down and decided to open a number of the floodgates and lower the level of the reservoir. There are 17 floodgates on the dam. At first they just opened a couple. Then they opened 10 or 12 of them at the same time.

What a sight! It seemed like as much water as Niagara Falls came tumbling though the gates. The level of the river went up 20 feet or more in places. Submersible bridge - one of our ways of getting out of township, was submersed. The water roared and sprayed and rushed down the river in huge white rapids. It was quite a sight.

Of course almost every Canadian family was down at submersible taking pictures. Photography of the dam is totally prohibited of course (for security reasons) so please don't tell the Indian government about the movies you will be seeing shortly showing the dam with the gates open.

While down at submersible taking pictures one night, we met two camel drivers who were willing to give us camel rides so Marg, I and all the kids had a good ride on the camel (if any ride on a camel can be considered good, that is). Camels are taller than you realize and these camels didn't have saddles – just a wooden basket affair which they use to tie on anything they want to carry. We sat on those. The scariest part of a camel ride is when it gets up and down. It kneels so you can get on – usually groaning and complaining as you climb on. Then it goes up – in three steps. First up on the front knees straight. Then completely up on the back legs. Then completely up on the front legs. As the camel does this, you go pitching backward, then forward, and finally upright. Then you bump and sway your way along the road hoping your ride will be over before the saddle falls off and you get killed in the fall. Then you realize you don't want the ride to be over because as soon as it is over, the camel is going to go through that business of back and forth again and you'll be thrown off then. However, it all ended safely for everyone in our family – no movies of that – just about 20 slides! Wait till you see our slides!

## Cultural Events in Kota!

During the past two weeks we have been seeing the sights in Kota. It started two weeks ago when we took the kids into Kota on a Saturday to see the museum and the zoo. We were pleasantly surprised at the museum. It is built into one of the walls of the city and has very interesting displays of sandstone statuary, old coins, weapons, historical information on Kota, miniature pictures (a famous Rajput style) and information about all the maharajahs of Kota. It is nicely set up with some displays outdoors and some inside. Admission is free and the guide was happy to explain anything that interested you.

We followed our museum visit with a trip to the Kota zoo. This is rather old and the smelly cages reminded us of a smaller version of Riverdale[35] a few years back. They had some interesting animals – a tiger of course, several kinds of deer and antelopes, and lots of water birds. We laughed to see one pen labelled "Yorkshire Pig". It didn't seem like a zoo animal to us. On the other hand, there were no monkeys, peacocks (actually there was 1 peacock) etc. in the zoo because they are seen so commonly in the countryside it is silly to put one in a zoo in India.

We completed a tour of Kota's cultural events by going to Rayman's Circus last night. It tours throughout India and is advertised as the largest circus in Asia. We bought "special class" tickets (1 step above first class) for 4 rupees (50¢) each and sat in the first row within five feet of the main circus ring. There was a big top and all the things you would expect a circus to have. The show took about three hours and was certainly bigger and better than any ever seen in Canada. There were literally dozens and dozens of really good performers. The costumes and equipment look a little shoddy by Canadian standards, but the talent isn't – far from it! It is just as you expect a circus to be but never is in Canada. This was the same circus we saw in Delhi in the fall but it was well worth seeing again.

## An Important Decision

Last week we made up our minds for sure. We had been asked to stay a third year and have been considering for the past three months whether or not to stay. We made our decision last week – we are not going to stay for a third year. In our letter to A.E.C.L. we said that for both personal and professional reasons we felt that two years was just the right amount of time to stay in India. We based our decision on our own feelings, of course, plus our observations of people who have come back for a third year after their home leave. Most of them seem rather depressed and seem to be just putting in

---

35   A former zoo in Toronto, Canada.

time until they can go home. This would be very bad for a teacher. As well as this, it seems that the little annoyances and frustrations that you meet in a different country are interesting the first year, you put up with them the second year, and they really bug you in the third year. So - we'll be coming home to stay next summer, at least for a couple of years until we can find another place to go!

## Visitor in Township

Last Sunday night an elephant was brought into township. Of course all the kids had a ride. Look for exciting films of that event too. Wow!

## Mr. Tranter's Lousy Students

If you thought cockroaches were bad - now hear this! It was recently discovered that at least half - and probably more - of the children in our school have head lice! You know what they are, don't you? Friendly little bugs that live in your hair. Apparently several of the Indian cooks and ayahs (nannies) have them and have passed them on to the children. The kids don't take it seriously at all. They go around saying things like, "My mother found some more on my head last night, how about you?". Of course it is a matter of much concern and even more consternation by the mothers in the community. At least one cook lost her job and all the girls and boys have suddenly developed a fondness for short hair. What about our kids? Margaret found several eggs in David's hair. None in Linda's or Jeff's hair so far, but don't give up - they may have them yet. You never saw so many freshly shampooed and specially treated heads in your life as there are around here. By the way, we are putting several lice in each envelope as a sample for you to see. I hope you noticed them when you opened the envelope. If not, they may have already hopped on your head!

## Now for a quick news round-up:

Slot Car Track: The slot car track is running nicely. I have rewound my first motor tonight for super speed. We're having lots of fun racing cars and working on the track several nights a week.

Laugh-In: Scripts for this year's Anushakti Laugh-In are coming along. We have the main outlines for the major productions finished and are working on the short skits. It should be lots of fun at Christmas.

School: We now own a beautiful Bell & Howell Autoload 16 m.m. movie projector. With luck, we'll show our first films next week. We order them from the Canadian High Commission in Delhi. They are almost all the National Film Board stuff.

We have a number of new pupils in our school or due on Monday. Three new Hydro families with a total of 10 children arrive this weekend. After they get here, our school probably reaches its peak number of kids - around 65.

The addition of the school is coming along slowly. It should be open in October. I wonder if we'll get a chance to use it before Christmas?

## Furniture from Kashmir

Yesterday we were in Kota and we picked up our shipment of coffee table and end tables from Kashmir from the railroad station. They arrived safely and we now have a very nice coffee table and two end tables in our living room and to take back to Canada. They are hand carved in a pattern of leaves much like Maple leaves. They are made of walnut. We hope they won't warp and crack like some cheap Kashmir stuff we have seen. They are from the same place that is making our dining room suite.

## Another Scorpion

While we were out for dinner the other night, our baby-sitter, a girl who lives two doors away, found a big black scorpion (the worst kind) in our living room. Like a true heroine, she called Jeff and David downstairs and they killed it with their souvenir canes. Actually they only injured it and put it in a can for us to see. That's the second scorpion in our living room in two weeks. We are also enclosing a scorpion in this letter for you to see. I hope it didn't hop out and hide in your bed when you opened the letter!

## Letters

Keep those cards and letters coming. We really look forward to mail. Particularly parcels with presents in them! If you want to buy anything for me, make it super-fast slot cars and hand controls.

Love, Bill, Marg, Jeff, Linda, David & Mandu.

Dear J-- & L--

     We were wondering if you would do us a favour. Hallowe'en is coming up next month and that will mean a big party here with lots of great costumes. Bill & I thought we would be Canadian Indians, but to do that we will need a headdress. Would you please go to the Lewiscraft store in Sheridan Mall and buy us an Indian headdress kit? We made two before but unfortunately didn't bring them with us. Buy a good one and air mail it to us. Wrap it really well, tape up the box securely first, mark it unsolicited gift and value it under $5.00. Write yourself a cheque from our account, J--, to cover the cost of the kit plus postage.

     Thank you,

     Bill & Marg

Greetings and we hope you had a happy Dusshera, Diwali and had fun celebrating Hallowe'en and Guru Nanak's Birthday! It's been a long, long time since our last newsletter but we'll try to make up for that with an interesting one. The large gap in letters is mostly due to an extremely busy month here, but more about that later. We hope everyone is well. All of us are fine except Margaret who has a slight infection but she is really quite all right except she has to take some antibiotic pills every once in a while. She isn't sick in bed or anything - just slightly grumpier than usual (if that's possible!). Well - on to other things - here goes with all the latest in township.

## Weather

The weather is pleasantly warm and sunny - every day. It is getting a little chilly in the pool except during mid-afternoon but it's just beautiful for everything else. In the 80's during the day, in low seventies at night.

## India Holidays

The fall of the year is big on holidays in this country. Here is a summary of what we've done on our holidays lately.

## Dusshera

Although we didn't get a holiday from school for this, this year we did celebrate by visiting the Dusshera fair in Kota. It was the most up-to-date thing we've seen in Rajasthan since we arrived!

There were all sorts of booths selling everything from material to guns and knives, toys, plastic ware, books, food, drugs, etc. There were also games of chance, sideshows, a few rides and lots of people. I've sent home a reel of movie film showing a little bit of the fair. I think it gives a good idea of typical Indians in the area. We all thoroughly enjoyed the fair although since we went with two other families we often drew more attention than the sideshows. As you can imagine, foreigners were a rarity at the fair - particularly for many of the rural folks who drove their ox-carts miles and miles to get there. We all stopped for pop at one booth and were soon surrounded by dozens of Indians interested in watching us drink pop - exciting, eh? A little later, I stopped to change the film in my slide camera and attracted a crowd of interested watchers who should have been watching a slightly broken-down dancing girl who was trying to get their attention at the sideshow beside me. Pretty good, eh? I'm more popular than a side-show!

## Diwali

Diwali is a really good Indian holiday. We took three days off school for that (Mon, Tue & Wed) and went on a 5-day trip to Udaipur and Mount Abu.

On a Saturday morning we left with the W--'s for Udaipur - about 200 miles west of here. Around lunch time we arrived at Chittorgargh - the chief city in the district where we live. It is famous for a huge fort that stands on the hill overlooking the city. We spent most of the afternoon exploring the fort with a guide (over 6 miles long - the fort, not the guide!) The fort was a famous bastion of the Rajput princes in their battles against the Moslems but it has an unfortunate history of defeats. The buildings are quite impressive and the history is most interesting - lots more about that with slides to illustrate when we get home.

In the late afternoon we continued our journey to Udaipur and arrived around 7:00 p.m. Udaipur is famous for its lakes and particularly for its Lake Palace Hotel - a Maharajah's palace built into the middle of a lake. So, of course, we stayed there. We got to the palace by boat and found that the hotel had very recently been renovated – in fact part was still in the process of being renovated. Our suite of rooms was quite acceptable. Two bedrooms with twin beds, a large living room, a dining room and two bathrooms plus two private terraces finished in marble and looking out over the lake. The accommodations were quite adequate. We spent the next day exploring Udaipur. It is a little larger than Kota and has several good antique stores that sell weapons, glassware, carvings, brass, etc. It would probably be a great place if you knew antiques, but we didn't so we didn't buy much.

On Monday we left for Mount Abu – a hill station about another 200 miles away. We arrived around supper time to find that there was supposedly no accommodation available in the whole place. Finally, the "Palace Hotel" gave us a room for the night. This hotel was supposed to be the best in Mount Abu but it was falling apart. The food was barely adequate and the hotel was rather dirty and poorly serviced but it was better than camping so we took it.

Mount Abu was in the midst of celebrating Diwali. The town was filled with tourists, souvenirs, fireworks and Canadians from Township! The kids found a roller skating rink and they all went roller skating that evening. Margaret and E-- W-- finally gave in and went roller skating too for a few minutes. We all had a good time.

Around noon on Tuesday, after some more sightseeing and shopping in Mount Abu with horse rides for the children, we left for Udaipur again. I-- W-- and I agreed to try an alternate route back that would save about 60 miles. It saved sixty miles all right but it didn't save any time! We travelled for about 60 to 70 miles over a road that was little more than a cart track across country, fording streams and easing our way over rocks and holes in what we laughingly called the road. At one point we forded a river that was deep enough to go over the front bumper of the car as we plowed through it but we didn't stall. In fact, both the W--'s Land Rover and our van got through very nicely with no damage or delays at all – not even a flat tire.

We returned to the Lake Palace Hotel Tuesday night – a nice change after the dump in Mount Abu. On Wednesday we spent more time shopping and sightseeing and left for township. Once more we took a short cut that took us on a slightly better, but still fairly rough road. We got back to township around 8:00 p.m. It was a good trip and we saw parts of Rajasthan we had never seen before.

Hallowe'en

As usual, Hallowe'en was big in Township. The kids all got dressed up and went trick-or-treating on the Saturday night. Then my class came down to the school for a big party.

On Sunday night the adults had a party with a dance band from Delhi and lots more crazy costumes. This year Linda went as a Rajasthani girl – an outfit that she can save and show when she gets back to Canada. David was a cave man and Jeff was a comic character called The Phantom. Marg and I were Indians with brown buckskin-type costumes and I had a headdress which I made from a kit J-- sent from Canada. It was a real weekend for parties. The kids and adults had a really good time.

## Guru Nanak's Birthday

Last Tuesday we had a day off for Guru Nanak's birthday[36]. We went on a picnic with another family down to an Indian village. I took two rolls of movie film of some pretty typical Indian villagers. Our lunch was observed by about 20 Indians. This is a great country if you like an audience. Wherever you stop, an audience just pops up or wanders in out of nowhere.

## School

Here are some of the reasons I haven't written lately: a new conversational French programme was just begun – taught by me??? A swimming programme for all pupils in my class during school hours has been organized. Films for the school are coming in regularly now from the Canadian High Commission. We get about 6 a week at all grade levels. These new programmes plus Hallowe'en parties (planning the class one was a big job!) and work and meetings on Laugh-In plus a lot of visitors to township have made the last few weeks hectic and it looks like the next few will be just as bad. In spite of that we'll try to write again soon. Please do the same!

Love from, Marg, Bill, Jeff, Linda & David (No cat – it disappeared while we were in Udaipur - sob!)

---

36  Guru Nanak was the founder of Sikhism.

Nov. 6/71

Dear J-- & L--

The Indian headdress kit arrived safely! Thank you very much. We made it and Indian costumes for Hallowee'en and it was a real success.

J-- would you please send us a copy of our bank statement <u>every</u> <u>month</u> from now on please? We have no idea how much money we have and we would like to know this before we plan our trip home.

Thank you again for the kit.

Love

Bill & Marg.

Christmas Newsletter 1971

Christmas Greetings!

Greetings from the Tranters. We hope that you have a very merry Christmas and we want you to know that we are thinking of you during the holiday season. All of us are safe and well and looking forward to our Christmas holidays. Our weather is still warm by Canadian standards. It is cool in the early morning - around 60 degrees - but it warms up every afternoon to between 75 and 80 degrees. There isn't any snow for Santa's sleigh but there isn't any frost on the car windshield either.

<u>Christmas Newsletter</u>                                    1971[37]

<u>Christmas Greetings!</u>
Greetings from the Tranters. We hope that you have a very merry Christmas and we want you to know that we are thinking of you during the holiday season. All of us are safe and well and looking forward to our Christmas holidays. Our weather is still warm by Canadian standards. It is cool in the early morning – around 60 degrees – but it warms up every afternoon to between 75 and 80 degrees. There isn't any snow for Santa's sleigh but there isn't any frost on the car windshield either.

We can imagine that you were wondering about our welfare as the India-Pakistan conflict developed. Of course, we are keeping up to date on the situation from many sources. It is a most unfortunate and extremely complex affair with both sides waging a partial war for many less-than-obvious reasons. There have been no signs of the war around here except for the consequences of a declared national emergency. We have black-outs every night with a minimum of light indoors and all windows heavily draped or covered with paper. The last four nights there have been air raid warnings but in all cases the planes sighted were Indian or a long distance away. We are in regular contact with the Canadian High Commission in Delhi and have been assured that if there is any indication whatsoever that R.A.P.P. Township might be considered a possible target area, we would be evacuated – probably back to Canada. This seems unlikely at present, however, so don't wait dinner for us on Christmas night!

As we look back over the past year, it has been a most interesting one. Since last January we have been to Bombay, Delhi, Kashmir, Jaipur, Udaipur, Agra and several other cities in Rajasthan. Our summer in Kashmir was most enjoyable. We look back to life on a houseboat, camping in the mountains, horseback riding and staying in everything from an Indian tourist hut to a luxurious hotel with fond memories. Several months ago we had an interesting trip to Udaipur where we stayed in the Lake Palace Hotel – a maharajah's palace in

---

37   As in the previous year, this Christmas newsletter was sent to a wider group of people with copies made on a spirit duplicator machine, some of which is reproduced here.

the middle of a small lake - and visited Mount Abu - a Rajasthan hill station resort. Again it was a trip of contrasts from a shabby, barely adequate hotel to luxurious surroundings from one day to the next.

This Christmas we hope to travel again if conditions permit. We plan to go by train to Bombay, then fly to Bangalore. From there we will fly to Madras. From Madras, it's back to Hyderabad and then Bombay again. We hope to spend two or three days in each city. We will come back from Bombay by train the day before school resumes.

Our school is playing an even more important part in our family life than usual this week. As well as Bill teaching and Jeff, Linda and David learning (we hope!) Margaret has been acting as a substitute teacher in the primary classroom. Mrs. W--, the regular teacher, has returned to Canada and we are just in the midst of finding a suitable replacement from one or more of the ladies in township. In the mean time, the whole Tranter family gets up and goes to the same school every day.

Our social life in township continues to be full and active. When you live within a few hundred yards of 30 Canadian families for more than a year, you make some very close friends. We are often invited out to dinner or for an evening of cards or conversation and we often have friends in. The whole community is so open and friendly that it is unusual to spend an evening at home without someone dropping in for a while. We also have a number of activities to keep our spare hours busy. We are working on a very ambitious variety show for February called Anushakti Laugh-In. It will be a series of songs, dances and skits about Canada and India. Our practices have been somewhat curtailed by the nightly blackouts but we're looking for ways to get around that too.

Our time in India is beginning to look very short indeed. Five months after Christmas we will fly out of Bombay and head for home. Our trip will include stops in Hong Kong, Tokyo, Hawaii, California and then across Canada to Toronto. We will probably be travelling for at least a month (June) and are still considering the possibility of having our car shipped to California and driving home from there. Until next July, then, when we'll return home and probably bore you to death with our slides and reminiscences, we wish you a very Merry Christmas and a happy and prosperous New Year from the whole Tranter family.

## Remember Us?

Well here we go. We finally got around to sending another letter. Why haven't we written? Well, there are several reasons:

1. E-- and I-- W-- left township for Canada when the war broke out so Margaret and another lady in township have taken responsibility for the primary class. This has meant a busier life for us all.
2. The big Anushakti Laugh-In production is coming up in a week and there are practices or planning meetings almost every night.
3. Progress reports went out from the school today - another few night's work.
4. We have been doing a lot of travelling. The whole Christmas holiday in South India and the January 26th Republic Day holiday (plus a few more days) in Delhi.

I'm writing this tonight because the township movie, which I usually show, has been cancelled because of the threat of power failures and bad weather. We have had rain all day - an unheard of thing in Rajasthan at this time of year. It must be the tail end of a hurricane or something.

By the way, I should be learning my lines for next week's show and Margaret should be working on props - she's the props lady - but we're doing this instead because of all our guilty feelings.

## The War

The war is over for all practical purposes anyway and it was a slaughter for India. It looks like East Pakistan will definitely become an independent Bangladesh and that there will be no more serious fighting for several years at least. It may drag on like the Arab-Israeli conflict with attempts to gain territory by either side from time to time but for Pakistan that will probably be some time in the distant future. So things are back to normal. The blackouts have ended. The air raid sirens no longer sound. The planes, trains, etc. are back to normal schedules. The men in township have stopped stock-piling gasoline for a fast retreat.

The war was very quiet in township. We saw:
No enemy planes.
No soldiers.
Heard no weapons.
Suffered no hardships - except regular blackouts every night for several weeks.

At least our kids can go back to Canada and say they lived through a war - if that is anything to be proud of.

## Margaret – the Teacher

Just before Christmas (mid-December) E-- and I-- W-- went back to Canada. Their reasons were complex but related to lack of job satisfaction on his part and his concerns for the safety of his family during the war. As a result I was suddenly without a primary teacher – with 1 hour's notice. Margaret began as a supply teacher on the following day and taught until Christmas.

Since Christmas Margaret and another local Canadian, J-- P--, have been sharing the teaching load. They both teach in the morning. They teach alternate afternoons. It seems to be working out quite well. Both teachers and children are finding it enjoyable – if hard work.

Now all five of us go to school every morning but only four of us return on every other afternoon. Of course Margaret is being paid for her services and the work isn't too hard with just 18 kids and 2 teachers so it seems to be working out pretty well.

By the way – in case you're wondering why we didn't send much news about the war – during the critical period the Indian government was imposing censorship on both outgoing and in-coming mail so we had to be rather careful not to include that sort of detailed information or the letter could have been confiscated or just conveniently "lost".

## South India

We had a very good trip to south India. The day we began all the planes returned to their regular schedules. Planes were on time and hotels were empty because all of the tourists had been scared away.

We went down by train to Bombay. Then left the same afternoon for Bangalore[38]. We spent about three days there sight-seeing, shopping, etc. and celebrating Christmas Day in our hotel room. We took a side-trip to see Mysore[39].

Then we flew to Madras[40] and spent 3 or 4 days on the east coast of India. Again we did lots of sight-seeing and shopping plus visits to the beach which is miles and miles long. The kids swam in the ocean – or at least paddled – the area is known for its sharks.

Then we flew to Hyderabad and again spent two days sight-seeing and shopping.

Then it was back to Bombay on New Year's Eve. We went to a very fancy restaurant for an 8 or 10 course gourmet meal and returned to our room not long after midnight and watched the square in front of the Gateway to India as literally thousands of Indians welcomed the new year and celebrated their "victory" over Pakistan. It looked just like Times Square in New York (only darker – the people that is).

---

38  Now known as Bengaluru.
39  Now known as Mysuru.
40  Now known as Chennai.

## Republic Day

At noon on Tuesday, January 25th, we left township to drive to Delhi. We arrived at about 9:45 p.m. Had a quiet evening and were up early the next morning to go to our reserved seats to view the famous Republic Day parade. It included quite a display of military might plus folk dance groups, youth groups, clowns, etc. etc. and a small air show. It lasted about three hours and was quite enjoyable.

Then we stayed in Delhi for three more days shopping and making some preparations for our trip home – at least gathering airline schedules. That will be our last trip to Delhi so we tried to buy any last souvenirs that we thought we might want.

On the way home we stopped in Jaipur overnight and Margaret ordered herself a ring which we should get next week. She decided to splurge with some of her teaching money and buy a Kashmir sapphire for herself. We arrived home in the afternoon on Sunday and started to get ready for both school and more Laugh-In practices almost immediately.

## Laugh-In

The Laugh-In show is going to last more than 3 hours on each of its two nights and includes a cast of 13 in a variety of skits, dances and songs. Most of the skits and song parodies were written by me (Bill) and I'm also one of the cast. Another township man and myself are also directing the whole show. It's a fantastically large job but a lot of fun too. It will all be over on the 13th (by the time you get this) so then we will rest easy for a while. I am enclosing a copy of the programme for your information. We'll bring slides and tapes when we come home to tell you more about it.

Well that's about all for now. A longer letter will come after the 13th of Feb. Hope all of you are well. How's the snow? Our weather's getting almost warm enough for the pool to reopen. Don't forget we like to see pictures once in a while too. Thanks for the Christmas presents. We decided to deliver yours personally when we get home because of the uncertainty of mail delivery because of the war.

Love, from Marg, Bill, Jeff, Linda & David

## ANUSHAKTI LAUGH-IN '72

### A CANADIAN PRODUCTION

**FRIDAY**

**FEBRUARY 11, 1972 at 8.00 P. M.**

CHILDREN 12 YEARS AND UNDER ADMITTED FREE

SEATS AVAILABLE FOR PROGRAM HOLDERS ONLY

**THIS PROGRAM IS YOUR ADMISSION TICKET**

**PRICE Rs. 2**

---

### PROGRAM—Part One

1. National Anthems
2. Age of Aquarius
3. R. A. P. P. Medical Centre
4. Snake Charmer
5. Air India's Jumbo Jet
6. Wooden Soldiers
7. Professor Hindi
8. Imported Food
9. Township Fashions
10. Duel Part I
11. R. A. P. P. Trio
12. Shamu, the Great
13. Walking in the Sunshine
14. R. A. P. P. Tourist Development
15. Pogo Stick
16. The Wistlers
17. Duel Part II
18. Poker Night
19. Monsoon Memories

INTERMISSION

---

### PROGRAM—Part Two

20. Charleston
21. Weight-Lifter
22. The Brassman Cometh
23. At the River
24. Professor Hindi
25. Pogo Stick
26. Duel Part III
27. R. A. P. P. Rural Round-up
28. A Letter Home
29. Indian Basket Dance
30. Bertha, the Water Buffalo
31. Uncle Booby Show
32. Dancing Class

INTERMISSION

---

### PROGRAM—Part Three

Z. A. P. P. Goes Critical

A Two—Act Play by :

William H. Tranter & Norman R. Anderson

Starring :

| | | |
|---|---|---|
| Herr Optimist | ... | William Tranter |
| Indira Madeira | ... | Irene Kears |
| Kingsberry Bearing | ... | Don Workman |
| Willie Pushbutton | ... | Mal Kears |
| Shorty Circuits | ... | Gerry Perreault |
| Alan Nytical | ... | Ed Chabrak |
| Hello Singh | ... | Norm Anderson |
| Ontario Heidi | ... | Jean Panke |
| Libby Heinz | ... | Jeanann Artiss |
| Campbell Kraft | ... | Julia Anderson |
| Nickie Mineral | ... | Marean Workman |
| Aggie Cultural | ... | Yvonne Keenan |
| Miss Niagara | ... | Felicity Harding |
| Business Manager | ... | Bill Artiss |
| Choreography | ... | Julia Anderson |
| Costumes | ... | Jane Borg |
| Lights | ... | Ron Vilim |
| Props | ... | Margaret Tranter |
| Sound | ... | John Mc Dowell & Bill Panke |
| Stage | ... | Alistair Glenn |

... and many others !

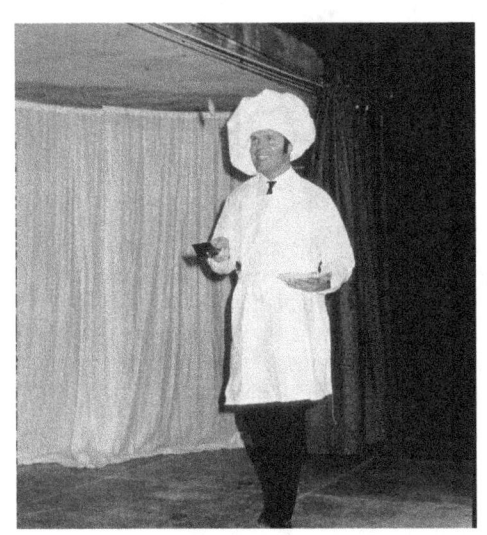

Hi! How is everyone? Thank you for your recent letters – those that sent some. Even when we don't get time to write letters we like to receive them. Now it's excuse time again with another set of reasons why it's been so long since the last letter. Would you believe?

1. We are very busy at school. We just had our Open House.
2. Bill and another fellow just spent a few evenings putting together a slide show with tape of the slides taken at Laugh-In time.
3. Our social life is becoming very busy – for reasons we shall mention below.
4. Getting ready to move half way around the world takes a lot of time.
5. Getting someone else moved half way around the world takes a lot of time – see below again.
6. The weather is very hot and most nights the thought of spending a couple of hours in the evening at the typewriter in the house is not pleasant.

BUT we are thinking of you regularly and we do remember all your names. (Or at least some of them – what was Marg's sister's name again – Grapes? Graves? Graze? Something like that wasn't it?)

## Our Trip to Goa

We had a great trip to Goa. We spent days just lying on the beaches eating fresh pineapple, oranges, bananas, etc. We had a really nice quiet holiday and got all rested up for the last big rush in township before we went home. We got some good pictures and saw some interesting sights such as the tomb of St. Xavier, statues of Vasco da Gama and other old churches and buildings dating back to the 1500's and still in use. Lots more about that when we get home – some really strange stories to tell about some of the strange beliefs of Goanese Christians.

We visited a light-house, watched fisherman unload sharks on the beach where we swam, went beach-combing at low tide and sailed from Goa to Bombay by boat on an overnight cruise.

Back in Bombay we stopped for souvenirs, bought school books and investigated airlines and bookings for our return plane tickets.

## Back in Township

Back in Township things have been busy. Another family and us have been arranging to have all the W--'s (former school-teacher) household goods either sold or sent back to Canada. They left their house during the Pakistan crisis and returned to Canada never to return. As their best friends we are helping to dispose of their goods. We've had three sales and spent days going through their belongings to get the total amount of their shipment down as low as possible so that it could be included in our shipment and that of the G--'s (another local family just gone home) at no extra cost. It was a big job. Now it is complete.

We have also just completed an Open House at the school where all the parents came to see what's going on. They were pleased and all the kids were busy showing their parents much of their work for the year. It was a lot of work preparing for it but well worth the time.

Preparing for next year has been a big job too. It includes ordering all school supplies for the coming year, corresponding with the newly hired teachers (a husband and wife team), putting in final expense accounts, etc. etc.

I (Bill) have also just completed a 15-page report on the status of school during the past year. The final typing still must be done for that.

With that plus looking after final repairs to the motorcycle and the car we've been very busy.

By the way, we've sold our freezer, motorcycle and washing machine to the new teachers (who will arrive the 3rd week of July). We are shipping our car directly back to Toronto. We are not shipping ourselves directly back to Toronto though. Attached you will find a dittoed letter that went out to most friends and relatives telling about our trip home. Get out a map and find the names of the places because you won't recognize some of them. It should be a great trip.

Now that we are getting close to going home (almost a month today) we are starting to get a lot of dinner invitations. Everyone wants to invite us for dinner one last time before we go home. We've been out to dinner or parties 5 of the last 8 days plus a banquet for Marg & Linda (Brownies) on another day.

## Our Dining Room Suite

We finally got our dining room suite from Kashmir about 3 weeks ago. We broke down and agreed to pay for it before we saw it and picked it up at the local railway station in Kota. We had to hire a truck to bring it in to township but we got it here. When we unpacked it we found some slight shipping damage that was repairable and generally speaking a very attractive dining room table, buffet and six chairs. The workmanship is quite good and we think it is well worth the money. Of course we won't really know until we see what happens after we have subjected it to the drastic change in climate and temperature in Canada plus the shipping home.

The movers dropped in to look over our stuff and say that we can easily get it in our allowable sea shipment of 250 cu. ft. So that is our biggest souvenir of India.

## Moving Out

The movers are coming to get our stuff on the third week of May. We leave here around the 3rd or 4th of June. We will start travelling light, but add stuff in the line of souvenirs, etc. as we travel. We intend to spend a fair bit of money on cameras, tape recorders, etc. in Hong Kong but this will be sent directly to our movers in Toronto to be cleared when we return. This is your last chance to ask for anything you want purchased in Hong Kong at about 50% of the Canada price (plus shipping and duty). If it's under $10.00 there's no duty and we can send it as a gift.

## Souvenirs

Several people have asked for Indian souvenirs (like you, Dad). Some of these won't be purchased until we're in Bombay on our way out so you won't get them for a while. There isn't much available locally. One souvenir we hope to buy is a hanging cane chair for the den[41]. They're cheap here and expensive in Canada. It will be just one more item in our Indian handicraft extravaganza rec room when we get home. Other features will be a concealed slide projector and screen and lockable doors so that we can trap unsuspecting visitors into watching a few thousand slides when they come to visit. Get those eyes checked now so they'll be in good shape for our return.

We don't know the exact date of our return but I think it's better that way. Then we can just suddenly appear on your doorstep one day. It will be much more dramatic.

Well that's all for now. Love from,

Marg, Bill, Jeff, Linda & David

---

41  We did get one.

Rajasthan, India
April 30, 1972.

Dear --

Hi! Remember the Tranters? We're coming home soon so we thought we'd better write a final letter from India before we leave. Here it is!

We just came back from the pool. The temperature outside is around 98 degrees in the shade. Inside, with a cooling "cus-cus" (a primitive kind of evaporative cooling system) the temperature is around 85 degrees but we're quite used to that by now. Every day is sunny and hot with few clouds in the sky and practically no rain. In the evening the temperature goes down to around 80 degrees. In our bedrooms it's cooler though with air conditioners on.

The school and our contract both finish for the year on May 31st. Then we'll pack up and drive to Bombay. There is a detailed itinerary of our trip home below. We'll be returning to our home in Mississauga (7208 Harwick Dr., Malton) and Bill will be going back to a job in Etobicoke. We look forward to returning to Canada. We'll enjoy the food, entertainment and luxuries that aren't available here. But we'll miss many of the good friends we have made and the perpetual summer climate. We'll come home with lots of good memories and quite a few souvenirs to remind us of India. Of course, you're invited to drop in and see our four million slides and hundreds of feet of movie film and our Indian handicrafts when we return.

On the way over here we travelled across Europe with stops in New York, London, Rome, Athens and Bombay. We will be going back via the Pacific. Here's our itinerary[42]:

June 4th - Leave RAPP Twp. to drive 750 miles south to Bombay.

June 5th - Arrive in Bombay and stay at the Sun 'N Sands Hotel for several days while we finish up local business.

June 8th - Leave Bombay for Bangkok, Thailand for several days of exploring and touring.

June 10th - Leave Bangkok for Penang, Malaysia.

June 12th - Rent a car and drive from Penang to Kuala Lumpur.

June 14th - Drive (or fly) from Kuala Lumpur to Singapore.

June 16th - Fly from Singapore to Hong Kong for a 5 or 6 day shopping spree and tourist visit.

---

42  It changed somewhat from what is listed here. See the Postscript section.

June 21st - Leave Hong Kong for Manila in the Philippines for several days.

June 24th - Fly from Manila to Port Moresby, Papua.

June 26th - Fly from Port Moresby to Honiara, Guadalcanal in the Solomon Islands for a week of lying on the beach, skin-diving and exploring a fairly primitive South Pacific island.

July 1st - Leave Solomon Islands for Nadi in the Fiji Islands for a look at a South Pacific island more geared for the tourist trade.

July 3rd - Leave Fiji Islands for Honolulu, Hawaii for several days of swimming and touring.

July 7th - Fly from Honolulu to Los Angeles for a visit to the West Coast of the U.S.A. including a couple of days at Disneyland touring and visiting relatives.

July 14th - Leave Los Angeles for Toronto.

Our air tickets after the first two stops will be booked as "open" tickets which means that you have paid for the flight but have no specific reservations. This means that we can change our length of stay at any point on our trip if we wish to spend more or less time than originally planned. The dates are only approximate. We'll get into Toronto within a week of the time shown above but we can't say the exact date.

As you can imagine, we are quite excited about our trip home and hope to take another two million slides on the way.

Our stay in India hasn't changed us much. The kids are bigger. Jeff will go into Grade 7 on his return. Linda goes into Grade 5 and David to Grade 3. I think we'll all appreciate Canada more but we'll also be much more restless to travel more. We're bringing our Volkswagen camping van home to Toronto and hope to use it for lots of exploring of North America during the next few years. We may even do a little bit during August of this year if business and professional responsibilities aren't too great. We look forward to seeing all our friends and relatives again. We'll probably be in to see you some time over the summer to get re-acquainted after our trip. Any time after about July 20th, feel free to drop in on us.

       With best wishes from India, Bill & Marg.

(this page intentionally left blank)

# Postscript

## The Trip Home

We left India in June of 1972, from Mumbai. We again took the opportunity to stop at some places in the way home, this time continuing east. Our destinations ended up being:
- Bankok,Thailand,
- Kuala Lumpur, Malaysia,
- Singapore,
- Papua, New Guinea,
- Honiara, Solomon Islands,
- Fiji,
- Darwin, Australia,
- Honolulu, Hawaii,
- Los Angeles, USA,
- and then home to Toronto. Canada.

After returning to Canada we moved back into our house in Malton that we had rented out during our absence. We were happy to reunite with our relatives and friends.

(this page intentionally left blank)

## RAPP Today

There were rumblings of India developing an atomic bomb as early as 1971 when Prime Minister Pierre Trudeau of Canada warned Prime Minister Indira Gandhi of India that the use of plutonium from the Canadian-supplied reactors for the development of a nuclear explosive device would result in a reassessment of Canada's nuclear cooperation with India.

In May of 1974 India's first atomic bomb was detonated in the Rajasthan desert. India later admitted that the plutonium for the bomb had been produced in a reactor. The Canadian government immediately suspended all nuclear cooperation with India and recalled the Canadian staff.

However, by that time the first RAPP-1 reactor was in operation and the RAPP-2 reactor was almost complete. India went on to build four more CANDU reactors without Canadian assistance, although the RAPP-2 reactor didn't start operations until 1981. At the time of writing there are seven reactors operating at the site with an eighth unit expected to come on-line in 2023.[43]

*Figure 3: A recent picture of RAPP. Photo credit: Wikipedia*

---

43 For more details see https://en.wikipedia.org/wiki/Rajasthan_Atomic_Power_Station

(this page intentionally left blank)

# What Became of the Tranter Family?

Bill Tranter continued teaching, becoming a principal and administrator, before moving into the field of management training, both with his own company as well as several management training and consulting firms. Divorced from Marg in 1975, he married Velta in 1984 (also a teacher). In 1993 he went to India to teach a course in Kota, Rajasthan and made a side trip to the RAPP Township. He passed away in 2008.

Marg continued teaching after the children left home, both part-time and full-time. She married Clare in 1993 and is retired and living in Cambridge, Ontario.

Jeff obtained a degree in Electrical Engineering and has worked in various engineering and management positions at high tech and software companies. Currently living in Ottawa with his wife Veronica, he has an adult son and daughter and three grandchildren and plans to retire in a few years. He made one business trip to Mumbai, India in 1999 and saw some of the same sights there that he remembered from years ago, including the Taj Mahal Hotel.

Linda acquired a law degree and practices law in Perth, Ontario residing just outside the town with her husband Jim (also a lawyer) and their two children who are currently in university. In 2019 they all made a trip to India, visiting several cities but also travelling to the RAPP Township and even meeting the family that now lives in the house that we lived in!

David earned a Ph.D. in Psychology and is an Associate Professor in the Social Work department of Lakehead University in Thunder Bay, Ontario. Married to Gail, they have three adult children.

I think it is safe to say that all of my family felt that our time in India shaped our lives forever. We gained a lifelong appreciation of other languages and cultures, an understanding of how lucky we are to live in a country like Canada, and a love of Indian food, music and culture.

(this page intentionally left blank)

# Alphabetical Index